Awaiting the Dawn

Dorcas Hoover

Cover Photo

Mark R. Valentino/D. Donne Bryant
Stock Photography

Christian Light Publications, Inc.
Harrisonburg, Virginia 22801

We present this account of the martyrdom of John Troyer and the events which followed with the prayer that God will raise up many others who will fearlessly carry the Gospel of Jesus Christ to the ends of the earth.

The Publishers

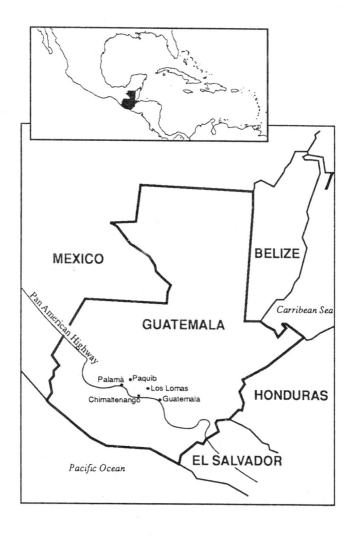

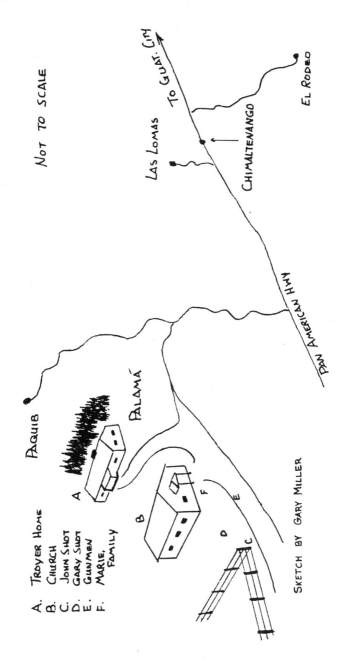

NOT TO SCALE

PAQUIB

PALAMÁ

A

B

F

E

D

C

A. TROYER HOME
B. CHURCH
C. JOHN SHOT
D. GARY SHOT
E. MARIE, GUNMEN
F. MARIE, FAMILY

SKETCH BY GARY MILLER

PAN AMERICAN HWY

LAS LOMAS

CHIMALTENANGO

EL RODEO

TO GUAT. CITY

PREFACE

The two summers my family served in Guatemala, when I was a child, ignited the spark of love in my heart for that picturesque country and its warm-hearted people. The intense interest and involvement of my father, Urie Sharp, in the missions there, fanned that spark.

In the summer of 1976, when I turned 16, we met John and Marie Troyer and baby John Ray at Chimaltenango. Years later, when I heard of the events that took place at Palamá, the Lord placed within my heart an inextinguishable desire to write the story. Several years later He confirmed it in the heart of Marie.

As a wife and a mother of three preschoolers, I intended to write only a short story, but my first written account of these events swelled well beyond the length I had intended. A year ago, I felt led to rewrite it as a small book. Many times I was uncertain how a section of the story should be worded or what should be included, but as I spread the manuscript before the Lord, the answer would come.

I shall always be grateful to the many who contributed to this book. If it would not have been for the support and prayers of my husband Jerry, the book would never have been written. The encouragement and counsel of those who reviewed the manuscript were priceless. Among others, Gary Miller, as well as my father and father-in-law, patiently reviewed each revision and gave helpful suggestions.

The main characters of this story and their relatives, friends, and fellow missionaries were extremely helpful in sharing memories, photos, and newspaper clippings, as well as in reviewing the manuscript for accuracy.

Working with this story and the people involved has deeply enriched my life. I will always treasure the friendship that developed with Marie during our visits in her home and through the countless phone calls and letters between us as she humbly shared her experiences.

Dorcas Yvonne Hoover

CONTENTS

Picture section in center of book

1

Shadows

Darkness draped its giant shroud over the jagged peaks of the Sierra Madres. The round moon hung low as if to illuminate the drama the night would unveil. The stars shone against the inky sky like slivers of broken glass.

Like a giant serpent, a rutted road humped its way from the Pan American highway to the ridge of a mountain eight miles away. Slithering through streams, twisting through cornfields and shadowy forests, the dirt drive snaked over razorback ridges and valleys. Slab wood shacks and cornstalk huts, with threads of smoke spiraling from their thatched roofs, dotted the dark mountain slopes. Up the shoulder of the mountain the road wound its way, teetering dangerously near the brink of ravines. The trail writhed on until it came to the shadowed forms of a lone dwelling, a chapel, and a school clinging to the spine of the mountain.

To the rear of the dwelling, an army of pine trees sighed and whispered in the wind. Beneath their swaying branches, a stealthy movement in the shadows betrayed dark forms lurking in the undergrowth, waiting for the lights of the isolated dwelling to be extinguished.

Had the curtains been drawn back from the window, one could have seen a glowing fire on the hearth.

To one side of the fire, a mother rocked her infant. Sweet tones of a lullaby accompanied the rhythmic squeak of the rocker. A wisp of dark hair escaped from the top of the pink blanket in her arms.

Marie's dark hair was brushed away from her pleasant face and twisted neatly under a black veil. Her large brown eyes were honest eyes with a touch of kindness and a serious look that hinted at a maturity beyond her 28 years. There was a trim youthfulness about her that denied mothering five children. Marie, with her spontaneous, outgoing ways, had grown up on a farm, handling a tractor as well as almost any boy.

Leaning back in his chair on the other side of the fire, John studied his Bible, his stockinged feet propped on the hearth. In the shimmering firelight, his sandy hair appeared golden. His clear eyes were serious eyes with the calm of a cloudless sky and a touch of humor within their depths. His love for the Guatemalan coffee was surpassed by his love for the Guatemalan people. John's love for people had been fostered by the years his parents spent as youth sponsors at their church. His father was a pastor, a grocer, and a butcher, and he had passed on his butchering skills to his son. Consequently, John butchered much of the mission's meat.

How special it is to be alone with John, Marie thought contentedly, gazing at her husband's rugged features. Moments alone with John were rare, as his hours were filled with visiting sick villagers, studying for Spanish sermons, and giving agricultural training. Besides his duties at Palamá, John pastored a second church, at Paquib (pah KEEP), a two-hour hike beyond Palamá. He also studied the Cakchiquel dialect.

The Troyers shared their house with John's assistant, Gary Miller, as well as Emiliana, a native Christian who had been hired to help Marie with the babies.

Since hearing of the death of Ruth's husband two weeks before, Marie considered time spent with John especially precious.

Ruth—like a dark cloud, the memory drifted into her thoughts, casting a dark shadow over her contentment. The smile on her lips evaporated. Ruth—dear friend! Only two weeks ago an accident snatched her young husband from her, leaving her with three small children. Marie shuddered. Seven years with John were not nearly enough. For several moments there was only the creak of the rocker and the crackling of the fire. Then softly her sweet voice carried the lines of a favorite hymn.

God's way is best; I will not murmur,
Although the end I may not see;
Where'er He leads, I'll meekly follow—
God's way is best, is best for me.

John looked up from his Bible. "That song is special to you, Marie."

"It's the prayer of my heart, John. That's why I wanted it sung at our wedding."

"Our wedding—it seems like a long time since we walked the aisle together," John mused, "and even longer since we were two teenagers stranded at the Guatemala City airport."

"Oh, the airport!" Marie laughed softly. "Do you know what an awkward feeling that was to be stranded in a foreign city with a former boyfriend?"

"No one met us at the airport because the message of our arrival hadn't been delivered. But I didn't mind being stuck with you," John confessed with a mischievous twinkle in his eyes. "I can still see you sitting on the suitcases to guard them while I went to flag down a taxi."

His tone grew serious. "I know God planned for us to go to Guatemala on the same flight—it wasn't just a coincidence. We had two dates at Bible school, then broke up after a letter or two, didn't we? What was it, three months after we came to Guatemala that we started dating again?"

"It was three months. You were stationed at Headquarters, while I was at the clinic here at Palamá," Marie replied dreamingly. "We didn't see each other very often, you know." Stroking the baby's soft hair, she asked, "Tell me again what brought you to Guatemala."

"Remember, I've told you how I went to Costa Rica with my minister when I was in high school," John began slowly with a faraway look in his eyes. "It was on that trip that I must have left part of my heart in Central America.

"When we visited William McGrath's children's home in Via Colon, I was touched by the 50 some abandoned children who reached out for love. There was something about the warmth of the Indian people, the poverty, and their pleas for missionaries that tugged at my heart. Two years later at Bible school I felt God drawing me to return to Central America."

Closing his Bible, he laid it on the floor beside his chair. "Last week I was asked why I am here when I could be earning a comfortable living back in Michigan. Money is not important to me; people are."

Marie glanced out the window. Often during

the daylight hours, she had watched dark-skinned, muscular men hoeing the fields of corn on the mountain slopes. Their wives hurried up and down the trail, balancing heavy baskets on their heads, sometimes with an infant bouncing in the shawl slung on their backs. Black, silky braids cascaded over blouses and ankle-length skirts, hand-woven with colors as brilliant as the birds that flew in the azure skies above the jade green mountains.

Years before, several villagers had walked for hours to reach the highway. There they had taken a bus to attend church services at the Conservative Mennonite Mission Headquarters in Chimaltenango, 30 miles away. "Please come to our village to teach our families about God," they had begged the missionaries. "We feel in our hearts what you teach is the truth." (The first service in the area of Palamá was conducted by the author's father, Urie Sharp, and Rogelio Pichiyá, in 1968.)

When missionaries came, they found the Mayan Indians living as their ancestors had lived in the sixteenth century. Though proud of their heritage and industrious, the Indians were trapped in a cycle of poverty, superstition, malnutrition, drunkenness, and illiteracy.

Most of the people teetered on the brink of starvation, subsisting on tortillas and black beans as they farmed their tiny plots by hand. Earning

6

approximately $200 a year, fathers spent their few coins on drink they bought from bootleggers. Half of the children died before the age of five from complications brought on by childhood diseases coupled with pneumonia and malnutrition. Their religion was a mixture of Catholicisim and paganism and included idol worship and witch doctors.

The remoteness of the wooded mountain made it an ideal hideout for guerillas who tried to recruit the villagers into their army. It was not unusual to see bodies sprawled at the bottom of a cliff, murdered by communist guerillas, right-wing extremists, or a death squad hired to settle a grudge. One night several months before, a young villager had been abducted from his home, leaving behind a sobbing wife and a six-week-old baby.

Various religious groups in Central America supported political activists trying to bring social justice through protests and bullets. But John stayed clear of politics. Marie could hear him teaching his flock Jesus' words: "Love your enemies, bless them that curse you, do good to them that hate you, and pray for them which despitefully use you" (Matthew 5:44). Marie could see the tranquility on the faces of the villagers who learned that peace comes through knowing God and not through using a rifle.

Though the primary goal of the missionaries

was to spread the news of the Gospel, they could not overlook the overwhelming poverty about them. With financial aid from churches in the United States and Canada, chicken houses and other agricultural projects were started by two previous missionary couples—Rogelio and Janet Pichiyá, and Mark and Norma Gingerich. John continued on with the projects and training they had begun, helping the Guatemalans to become self-sufficient. He taught improved, scientific methods of farming, such as the use of fertilizer, to increase the meager incomes.

John and his co-worker, Gary Miller, spent hours keeping the rugged road passable and maintaining the vehicles that were battered by the rutted road. They sat at the bedside of the sick and made ambulance runs to the hospital with critically ill patients. When traveling to Chimaltenango for supplies twice a month, they frequently hauled loads of fruit to the highway for the villagers.

Nearly every meal was interrupted by a knock on the door—by some villager who sought John's counsel on crops, a spiritual struggle, or a decision he faced. The Indians, with their sensitive nature, could feel John cared about them, and they had learned to trust his advice.

A schoolhouse had been built to educate the youth and to hold reading classes for the adults. Marie held classes for the women in nutrition, hygiene and sewing.

For two years before her marriage to John, Marie had used the porch of the house as a makeshift clinic. She had given shots to combat pneumonia and infections and had treated many machete wounds.

By their service, the missionaries demonstrated God's love to the Indians and told them more about the One who died for them.

As Marie reflected now, she could see the smiles on the faces of the villagers, smiles that were as warm as the fires over which they baked their tortillas. She could feel the hug of a grateful young mother saying, "Thank you! Thank you, Maria, for coming to tell us about God. Our hearts are free from superstition and fear since God lives in our hearts. Our husbands earn more money from their crops since John showed them how to farm better. Our men have stopped drinking and they use their money to buy clothes for the children. And you are here to help us when we are sick. We can read God's Word since you came to tell us how. Oh, thank you, thank you, Maria, for coming to Palamá!"

It was reward enough.

Marie looked away from the window. "They need you here, John." Her voice was soft and full of emotion.

John sighed. "That's what I told Dad when I called him from the phone at Headquarters

Tuesday night. He worries when he hears of all the guerilla activity taking place here in Guatemala. I told him, 'Dad, don't worry about us. We'll leave the country if there is any threat of danger. We don't bother them and they don't bother us.'"

Marie studied John's face. Were his tense facial muscles evidence of worry that he tried to hide? "I know God wants us here at Palamá," she said, "and He won't allow anything to happen that's not His will. Yet it still scares me sometimes, John. We are so isolated here—two hours from the main road, with no telephone, no police, and no nighttime radio contact with Headquarters." Dropping her eyes, she half-whispered, "And . . . I just can't forget my dream."

"Don't think about it, Marie, please."

"I can't help it, John. I can see it so clearly . . . all those—"

"Don't, Marie! Let's head for bed. Four o'clock will be here before we know it. We don't want to keep the other missionaries waiting. They are expecting us first thing in the morning to help put the roof on the building at El Rodeo. We've got a big day ahead if we plan to go on to Guatemala City to visit with Mark and Norma Gingerich."

John stifled a yawn, stretched, and rose from his chair. Pulling back the curtain, he remarked,

"The moon is awfully bright tonight. I hope—"
Seeing the look of anxiety in his wife's eyes, he
swallowed his words of apprehension. Stroking
the velvety head of his infant daughter, he
whispered, "Sleep well, little love." Then, turning, he stirred the coals and banked the fire for
the night.

"I was hoping to finish my letter to Mother
and Dad while the children are sleeping and
everything is quiet, but. . . ." Marie's voice died
away as she recalled Ruth, alone tonight, with
three small children. "I'll finish it another time."

Gently she picked up the sleeping infant and
carried her to the bedroom. Tenderly she laid
Karen in her crib and tucked the blankets around
her.

Turning to the other end of the crib, Marie
adjusted Sharon's blanket. "Sleep on, precious
ones," she murmured. Nights had been short the
last five and a half months since the birth of the
twins.

In the children's bedroom, three-year-old
Timothy's freckled face lay against his favorite
blanket which he held in his little arms. In the
next bed, moonlight was shining on John Ray's
light hair. *He couldn't look more like his father,*
Marie thought as she pulled the blanket over her
six-year-old son. Four-year-old Marilyn clutched
her doll, her long brown braids sprawled across
the pillow. All was peaceful. If only . . . if only it

would last.

Marie blew out the light.

While the family slept, the flickering light of a lamp cast eerie shadows upon the kitchen wall. At the table, Gary sat with his chin propped in his hands. His eyes held the look of one in deep thought. Dark hair fell across his forehead. His countenance was one of composed fearlessness and strength.

He could hear Timothy cry out for a drink of water, and he heard the occasional wail of a baby.

A throaty growl from the direction of the dog house was echoed by the startled crow of a rooster. Gary's eyes darted to the dark shadows beyond the kitchen window. Was there a movement in the bushes?

He reached out to close the curtains. On most nights he liked the curtains open to see the silver disk of the moon above the pines, and the stars that seemed closer and brighter than at home in North Carolina, but not tonight. He could almost feel eyes watching him from the darkness.

Gary could not shake the sense of foreboding that gripped him. "Why can't I relax and go to bed?" he asked himself. The hands on the clock showed 11:25.

He glanced at the poem he had just completed about his childhood memories. "What have I accomplished in my short 21 years?" he asked himself.

In his mind's eye he could see his family circled around him at the airport six months before. He could see his mother dabbing at her eyes with her handkerchief. He could feel the weight of his pastor-father's hand on his shoulder as he prayed, "We put our son in Your hands as he leaves us to do Your work. We ask that Your will may be accomplished." Gary could feel the tug at his jacket as his youngest brother voiced the question everyone was thinking. "You'll come home again, Gary, won't you?"

Intently, Gary penciled the date, September 13, 1981, in the upper right-hand corner of his poem. *If something should happen during the night, those who find this will know it was my last work,* he thought as he extinguished the lamp.

2

Midnight

The stillness of the night was shattered by the urgent yelping of the dog. Instantly, Marie was wide awake. Her body tensed as she strained to hear any sign of what had alerted the dog. Was an intruder prowling outside the house? She could hear the heavy breathing of her husband beside her and the rhythmic "tick . . . tick . . . tick" of the alarm clock. In the dark room, the pale green glow of the lighted dial showed ten minutes before midnight.

"CRASH! SMASH! BOOM!" The front door groaned under the blows that threatened to break it down, and the whole house seemed to shudder.

"Get out of the house!" frenzied voices shouted in Spanish. The hatred in the tones sliced the air like sharp machetes. "Get out immediately! Get out! Get out with your hands up!"

14

Icy fear gripped Marie's spine. John sat straight up in bed. "Can you see who's out there?" he rasped, leaping out of bed.

Trembling, Marie eased toward the window. She peered through the curtain. A chill shot through her body. There was only glass between her and three masked men who were pacing on the porch, hacking at the door with their gleaming machetes. Only their dark beady eyes could be seen from behind the holes in their hoods.

Marie drew back with a gasp. The brilliant, silvery light of the moon illuminated the lane directly in front of the porch where six or eight dark forms lay, the muzzles of their guns pointing at the house. It was exactly like her dream.

John had come up behind Marie and was looking out over her shoulder. "Get dressed, Marie. Quickly!" His voice was edged with urgency.

Marie jerked a dress over her nightgown.

Three gunshots exploded outside the house, splintering through the front door.

Closing his last shirt button, Gary ran down the hall to John's room. With a quick knock, he burst into the room, wide-eyed and breathless. "What will we do, John?"

"Is there any chance of slipping out the back door and going for help?" John wondered as he tied his shoes.

"It's too risky." Gary shook his head. "These

men have guns. I'm sure they've got the place surrounded."

The door groaned under the blows. It could not hold up much longer. Gary glanced out the window. "I think we should pray."

The three knelt at the side of the bed.

From outside the window came the agitated shouts. "Get out! Get out immediately! Get out!"

"Oh, Father!" Gary cried. "Protect us if it is Your will. Please keep the dear little children safe. Forgive any sin in our lives . . . and," he added softly, "if a life must be taken, let it be mine."

The lock was slashed from the door, and fell to the floor with a crash. The door creaked open.

"Sirs!" John called out the window. "We'll give you anything we have if only you'll spare our lives!"

"Come out!" the reply came. "No one will be killed, we promise. You have ten minutes to be out here with your hands in the air."

Marie searched John's face. Even in the darkness, she could see his slumped shoulders and the anguish in his eyes as he looked at Gary. There was no escape. There was no option. Marie felt like a trapped rabbit with hunters and yelping hounds tunneling their way into her burrow. "Trapped . . . trapped . . . trapped," the clock seemed to chant. "Trapped . . . trapped . . . trapped."

John took Marie's hand. "Let's get the children. Gary, call Emiliana."

Marie moved slowly, clearing her thoughts. The night was cold. They would need blankets to wrap around the little ones. If only she could wake up to find it had all been a bad dream. But she knew it was for real. She could hear Gary pounding on the hired girl's door, shouting, "Hurry, Emiliana! We've got to get out of the house!"

Carrying the sleeping babies, the young couple led their pajama-clad children into the dark living room. The door sagged on its hinges. Moonlight bled through the bullet holes and the gaping hole where the door handle had been.

"I'll go out first," Gary volunteered bending to pick up Marilyn. He stepped into the open doorway, silhouetted against the night, shoulders back and head erect.

Immediately Gary was surrounded. Every direction he turned, he looked down the barrel of a gun.

"Manos arriba! Manos arriba!" (Hands up!) The voices rang with authority.

Gary wrapped Marilyn's small arms around his neck and held his hands above his head as the terrorists searched him. The child sobbed and clung frantically to Gary's neck.

"Hurry, John, please!" Where was he? "Don't make the men wait!"

"I'm changing my shirt," John called from the bedroom. "This one has a button missing."

Why is he worried about a missing button at a time like this? Marie wondered. *Is he subconsciously stalling for time?*

The men were nearly finished searching Gary. Marie thought quickly. It would be unwise to irritate them by making them wait. "Emiliana, I'll take Sharon and John Ray. You bring Karen." Timothy sat on the floor, rubbing his eyes and blinking, not quite awake. "Honey, wait for Daddy."

Holding her baby tightly to her, Marie took John Ray's hand and stepped out onto the porch. The cold night air hit her face. Shivering, she pulled the blanket tightly around the baby. She looked up to see gun barrels glaring at her from every direction. Her knees shook as the men closed in to search her. She could smell wood smoke on their clothing and could hear their heavy breathing.

Would I recognize any of the faces under those masks? Marie wondered as she eyed the three hooded men with their naked machetes. *Who are these men and why are they here? What do they want with us?*

Satisfied that Marie was unarmed, the gang turned to Emiliana. John stepped through the door, carrying Timothy. He pulled the door shut behind him.

"Sit on the floor." The gruff voice was edged with impatience. Turning to see who had spoken, Marie spotted the spokesman. Attired in camouflage fatigues, a young Indian paced restlessly, his gun cradled in his arm convenient for quick access. Marie could see in his eyes the hardened glint of an animal eyeing its prey as he watched his comrades search John.

This was the season that normally brought rain every night, yet the sky was unusually clear tonight. Stars twinkled brightly overhead. God, too, was looking down on the little defenseless group, Marie was sure.

Like the floodlights of a stage, a full moon illuminated the scene. Besides the three masked gangsters in civilian dress, there were approximately seven men uniformed in camouflage green, berets on their raven-black hair and guns strapped to their shoulders.

The spokesman stepped toward John. "Do one of you have the key to the vehicle?"

"I've got them." Gary pulled a ring of keys from his pocket and handed them to the spokesman.

A fragment of hope wove itself into Marie's heart. *Perhaps they'll take the Blazer and leave,* she hoped silently.

"Is there any gasoline?" The gunman's steely eyes rested on John.

"It's in the shed behind the house." John's

voice held a quiet calmness.

An aggressive man who appeared to be the commander barked orders, and the gangsters split up, heading different directions as if carrying out a well-rehearsed drama. The spokesman and a comrade stood near the family, their guns poised.

Several men worked under the hood of the Blazer. Others carried cans of fuel from the shed standing ten feet behind the house and began dousing the vehicle. As the gas gurgled and splashed from the cans, Marie felt the fragment of hope unraveling within her. The last route of escape was about to go up in smoke. Even with the Blazer it took almost two hours to reach the highway.

Fuel sloshed as it hit the walls of the shed and streamed down its sides.

Several men carrying gunny sacks pulled the door open and barged inside the house. The young mother winced as she heard the creaking of drawers, the shattering of glass, the crashing of furniture, and the splashing of fuel. Marie tensed as she thought of the photo albums, the afghan John had given to her when they were dating, and the heirloom quilts the grandmothers had lovingly stitched for the babies. Strangers were rummaging through her possessions, preparing to burn them, and she was helpless to stop them.

Will we even need our possessions after tonight? Marie wondered mutely. Suddenly it mattered little that her dishes were being broken, that strange hands were rummaging through her drawers, even that all their earthly possessions might soon go up in flames. Furnishings could be replaced; lives could not. *If we escape this night with only the clothes we are wearing, I'll be ever so grateful.*

She worried about John, remembering her dream. "You don't think they'll shoot you, do you?" her voice was barely a whisper.

"Nah," John shook his head, trying to appear nonchalant. "Why would they want to do that? You worry too much."

"I'm so cold, Mommy." John Ray snuggled against his mother, shivering in his pajamas.

"Sirs," John spoke to the guards. "My sons are cold. Could we please have several blankets from the house?"

The young Indian's eyes narrowed as his lips curled into a sneer. "Now you know how we feel! We don't have enough blankets for our children either!"

John and Gary were taken into the house at gunpoint, by turn. Each was asked to locate his camera and binoculars. "Hurry!" the terrorist shouted, kicking Gary. When John and Gary returned. blankets were carried from the house, and the children were wrapped in them and cuddled in the arms of the adults.

The spokesman faced the little group again like a cat preparing to torment its captured mouse. "You have been deceiving the people, and we have come to put a stop to it!" His voice was determined, icy, metallic. "You have put false ideas into the people's heads."

John cleared his throat. "In what way are we deceiving the people?" he questioned, weighing his words carefully, as if they were the match that could light the dynamite of the terrorists' displeasure. "What ideas have we taught them that are false?"

"You are teaching them evil lies, things that aren't good for them!" the leader retorted. "You know!"

"We have no desire to deceive the villagers. We have come to bring your people the truth of God's Word—"

"You talk to the villagers against the guerillas," the gunman cut in impatiently.

John remained mute. Sweat dripped off his face. In the tension and fear of the moment, the Spanish words didn't register.

"He says we talk against the guerillas," Marie whispered.

"We don't become involved with politics." John's quiet voice contrasted with the loud angry words of his interrogator.

The terrorist kicked at a rock with the scuffed

toe of his boot. "I don't believe that!" He fingered a clip of bullets. "What do you teach the people?"

"We teach God's Word," John replied. "We teach the Bible."

"I don't believe it!" the gunman retorted. "That's not true. We know you teach them evil lies." Intently he studied his captives. He glanced toward the men preparing to burn the Blazer, then continued his accusations.

"You are rich and we are poor! How much money do you have in the house?"

"About $160," John replied after a quick mental calculation.

Digging into his pocket, the terrorist produced a penny. "Look! All I have is one penny in my pocket. I am poor! That's why we have come. We are the Army for the Liberation of the Poor."

With his dark eyes flashing, the terrorist waved his costly rifle. "If anyone asks who was responsible for this night, tell them that! We are the Army for the Liberation of the Poor. We are not killing people for the fun of it. There is a reason!"

Marie's face turned as white as the baby's shawl. "Dear God! They intend to kill!" Feeling weak, she leaned against John. *So they claim to be guerillas*, she thought, recalling all she had heard about the terrorists. The United States government had given aid to the Guatemalan

Army to help combat these communist-backed terrorists who tried to topple the Guatemalan government and who committed acts of terrorism against the rich. Since they assumed all foreigners were rich and exploited the poor, they disliked foreigners as well. Shuddering, Marie recalled hearing of the ruthless tortures, murders, and kidnappings the guerillas had been credited with. "God have mercy."

The interrogator leaned down toward Emiliana. A look of fear flashed across her dark face. "You are an Indian. Aren't you poor? You are tired of being oppressed by the *gringos*, aren't you?"

"Sure we are poor," Emiliana answered boldly, gathering courage. "But we believe in getting out and working with our hands to earn a living. The missionaries haven't oppressed us. They have helped us."

Rebuked by a fellow Indian, the gunman turned again to the missionaries. "You are rich Americans taking advantage of us poor Indians!" he shouted.

"How unfair!" Marie wanted to shout. Instead she sat meekly beside her husband, her eyes shining with tears as she thought about the clinic, the school, the sewing and health classes, the clothing and quilts they had distributed, the unpaid loans. She felt as though she had been kicked in the stomach by one for whose people they had sacrificed so much. Her heart cried out, *These men don't really know us and all we've done here at Palamá, or they couldn't talk like this.*

"It is because we care about your people that we have come to your country," John began quietly. "Can't you see it is because we love them that we have tried to improve their lifestyle? We are here to give, not to take." It was beyond the grasp of the terrorist that anyone would come to his country for any purpose other than for personal gain. His face seemed blank and uncomprehending.

"Even your dog has a house!" the spokesman growled. Pointing a finger at the dripping Blazer, he continued, "You have a car, and our children don't even have shoes! Is that fair? Is it?"

Gary could sit still no longer. "Sir," his voice was patient, yet firm. "Sir, the possessions we have make it possible for us to serve your people. If it were not for our four-wheel-drive vehicle, we could not aid your people in this remote location. Our primary goal is to tell the people about God, but we've been helping them materially as well."

"We know you are rich Americans taking advantage of the poor Indians," the spokesman repeated obstinately.

"Sir, we've been trying to tell you we are here

to help your people. We have come to share with them. We've been giving interest-free loans to help the people finance their crops." John's gentle voice was filled with emotion. His tense facial muscles were beaded with sweat. He did not mention the $700 he had personally lost through unpaid loans, practically draining his own bank account.

"Where do you get your money if you don't get it through exploiting the natives?" the gunman demanded.

"The churches in the United States care about their brothers here, too. They want you to learn to know God. They send us a small salary each month to help pay for our expenses such as fuel and groceries. The churches in the United States paid for the house and the vehicle. Their women made quilts and clothes for the villagers. The churches financed the chicken houses and other projects to try to help the villagers earn a better living. There was no gain for them or the missionaries other than the joy of seeing changed lives and helping their brothers step out of poverty."

A glimmer of sympathy sparked in the Indian's dark eyes, then flickered and became cold as he continued his tirade of accusations. "You are rich Americans and we are poor," he said coldly, with the ring of a judge pronouncing sentence.

While the relentless interrogation continued,

the house was emptied of everything that appeared to have value and could easily be carried away. Cameras, flashlights, recorders, a chain saw, the two-way radio were brought from the house and piled in front of the porch.

The spokesman was joined by the aggressive commander who had overseen the ransacking of the house and the dousing of the Blazer and shed. His eyes held the cold, merciless glare of a panther. His mouth was frozen in a scowl, etched there by the chisel of bitterness.

Pacing restlessly in front of the porch, he taunted, "How do you feel about what we are doing? Is it fair?" He pointed his gun toward Gary and snapped off the safety menacingly. "How does it make you feel?" His cruel eyes bored into John.

"Naturally we feel very sorry for what is taking place." John's voice was soft.

As the house grew silent, heavy footsteps approached the door. With a groan, the bullet-scarred door opened. As the remaining gangsters shuffled out of the house with bulging sacks over their shoulders and disappeared down the trail, John Ray cried out, "Mommy, they are taking our things away!"

"Hush, darling, I know." Marie pulled her son close. *I wonder what they've left behind*, she thought mutely.

How grateful she was that the babies slept

soundly. Two screaming infants could aggravate their captors.

Marie glanced at John's watch. It was 1:00. It would be 2:00 in Missouri. Her family would be asleep in their warm beds. Didn't they know their daughter was facing one of the most heart-rending moments of her life?

Fuel gurgled from cans as again it was splashed over the sides of the Blazer. Sloshing, splashing, gushing, the fuel drenched the vehicle and lay in puddles beneath it.

Several men sloshed fuel onto an old rug. A match was pulled from a pocket as two men bent to shove the rug under the Blazer, only several feet from where the little group sat.

"Wait!" John cried. "It'll explode! We'll have to move away!"

"You'll stay right where you are," the spokesman replied flatly.

"Please! It's too dangerous to be this close. Please let us move!"

The spokesman searched the face of the leader. "Okay, get going, but only several feet." He fingered his gun in readiness as he herded his captives down the hill.

Scarcely had the missionaries settled on the dewy grass above the church, when the flaming rug was flung under the engine of the Blazer. With a roar, flames leaped through the grill and the open hood, engulfing the vehicle with a howl. Gasoline sizzled as tongues of flame licked at the paint and devoured the seats. The windowpanes exploded into a million flying shards of glass.

Flames lunged toward the sky, leaping and gyrating like a hundred dancing savages, twisting and contorting, painting the night a brilliant orange. Black plumes of smoke billowed above the pines, spewing sparks toward the stars.

Every muscle in her body tensed as Marie waited for the explosion which would shoot jagged bits of twisted metal like hunting arrows in every direction. But it did not come.

As Marie gazed at the fire, she saw a memory in each flame. She saw memories of hurried, bouncing, sliding rides in the Blazer to save the life of a dying child. But now the Blazer was going up in smoke.

Behind the house, a flaming match was tossed on the fuel-soaked shed. With an angry hiss, clouds of smoke exploded from the building. Crackling flames engulfed the shed, reaching ravenously toward the fuel-saturated house only ten feet away.

3

"No! Please, No!"

A voice with an edge of steel sliced into Marie's thoughts. "Okay, leave the children here and come with us."

Marie stifled a scream. Her face blanched. Tears spilled down her cheeks. It was a mother's nightmare. "No!" she sobbed. "Don't take them away from us! Please don't take our children away!"

The spokesman looked from the crying infant in the distraught mother's arms to the small son clinging to her skirt. He fingered his gun indecisively as he gazed thoughtfully at the burning Blazer.

All her motherly instinct welled up within Marie like a great fountain of anguish. "Not our children! Oh, don't take our children away!" Her eyes grew large and shimmered with tears as she hugged her baby against her.

What did they plan to do with the children?

What would they do with her and John and Gary? Tears coursed down her cheeks and dripped onto the baby's blanket. "No! Please, no!"

Wordlessly the spokesman watched the flames devour the vehicle. His stubby fingers combed and recombed his raven-black hair.

Finally he turned to the missionaries. "Come with us," he ordered tersely.

Not risking to ask who was to come, the adults picked up the children and followed the gunman and the commander down the slope to the church house.

Above the door hung the hand-lettered sign: *Iglesia Evangelica, La Nueva Jerusalen, Mision Menonita* ("Evangelical Church, The New Jerusalem, Mennonite Mission").

Marie thought of the smiling villagers who had crowded into the building only hours before to take part in the Sunday evening service. Men had removed their straw hats while women pulled their hand-loomed shawls tightly around their shoulders. Lantern light had flickered over the open song books and radiant faces.

After an inspirational evening of vibrant testimonies from the audience, John had closed the service with a favorite verse, his personal testimony: "For to me to live is Christ, and to die is gain" (Philippians 1:21). The memory struck Marie's heart. "To live is Christ . . . and to die

. . . to die is gain." Now the church was dark, and the villagers were hiding in the cornfields in helpless horror.

"Set the children down," the gunman snapped, pointing a stubby finger at John and Gary. "Stand over there." He gestured with the barrel of his gun to the fence 20 feet away.

Marie froze. The realization of what was about to take place stabbed her heart like the blade of a machete. "You can't kill them!" she cried in anguish. "You can't!"

"Put the children down!" the gunman snarled.

Gently, Gary set Marilyn on the damp grass beside her mother. With purposeful step, he walked silently toward the fence.

John bent down to set Timothy in front of Marie. Timothy's small arms locked around his father's neck in a frantic embrace. "Daddy! Daddy!!" he screamed.

As John unlocked the little arms and pulled away, his eyes met Marie's. His eyes, always calm, reflected now the dark turmoil of a spring thunderstorm. They held clouds of anguish. In that fraction of a minute that his eyes were riveted to Marie's, they seemed to be signalling a hundred messages. "You know how I love you, Dear. It tears me up to leave you," they seemed to tell her.

Marie drank in those priceless seconds, engraving his blue eyes, his rugged features, and blond hair onto her heart. Her face turned pale. "John—" She caught his hand. There were so many things she yearned to tell him. *Don't go . . . I love you . . . We need you . . . I'm sorry about the time.* . . . But no words came from her quivering lips.

"To the fence!" the terrorist's voice held a metallic ring.

John pulled his hand from his wife's and walked toward the fence. His shoulders were bowed, not from fear for himself, but from the weighty knowledge that he was leaving his family alone and unprotected.

Marie found her voice. "John! Don't go! They'll shoot you!"

"Daddy! Daddy! Daddy!!" Timothy shrieked, reaching for the retreating figure.

Never had Marie felt more helpless. Never had she longed more for the strength of John's presence, but they were leading him away like a lamb to the— "No! God, don't let them!"

As the terrorist raised his gun, the last thread of hope within Marie snapped. A torrent of anguish and fear such as she had never felt washed over her like a tidal wave.

Compelled by terror and loyalty, the little mother cried out, "Sirs! Don't kill them! We'll leave tomorrow if you'll only let them go!" she ended in a sob.

The commander whirled to face her. He

smiled a cruel, hard sneer. "You'll leave tomorrow, will you?"

The gunman looked to the leader. "Can't we let them go?"

"Shoot," came the stony reply.

Marie buried her face in the baby's shawl. "Oh, God! I can't bear to watch!"

A red streak of flame flashed from the gun barrel as the gunman shot from the hip in John's direction. The thunder of the explosion blasted the moonlit stillness, shredding Marie's heart into a thousand pieces.

She hardly dared to look, yet she couldn't bear not to. Fearfully, she lifted her head.

He stood! John stood! His tall form silhouetted against the darkness, the silver moonlight reflecting on his light hair. For a fleeting moment, Marie forgot everything in the pride that welled up within her. He was her husband, her husband John that was standing so bravely before the open-barrelled gun.

A thread of hope spun itself across her heart. Perhaps they would not kill him. Perhaps, oh, perhaps this was only a game meant to intimidate John into leaving. She desperately hoped it was.

Again the terrorist leveled the gun.

"No!" Marie cried. "Please don't!" she sobbed softly.

Another flash, and another bullet tore through the darkness.

Still John stood. "Please, sirs, have mercy!" His voice was soft, gentle, pleading. His broad shoulders hunched forward as if to protect himself from the bullet that would rip through his body any second. "Have mercy!"

Gary stood numbly, clenching and unclenching his fists. If only he could stop them! John was a husband, a father. His family needed him! But all Gary could do was to pray, "God! Your will be done! Your will be done . . . God, Your will be done!"

With a thunderous crack, another bullet slashed the night with a trail of fire. Still John stood. Marie could hear him praying aloud, sobbing softly, pleading for mercy. "Please, sirs, please, have mercy!"

Again the gun was leveled. There was a tense moment of silence.

Marie gathered courage. "You can't kill him. You just can't! He has five small children. Oh, have a heart!"

"Daddy!" sobbed the children. "Daddy, Daddy-y-y-y!"

The gunman hesitated, a cloud of uncertainty crossing his face.

The leader whirled to face Marie. His eyes narrowed into slits. His voice was cold, hard, and menacing as he spit his words from between his yellow teeth like a snake spitting its venom. "Be quiet, woman!"

Eyes brimming with tears, Marie lowered her head and swallowed the words that pushed at her lips. She must be careful not to irritate the terrorists. Her children needed a mother. She pressed the little faces against her to shield them from the dreadful view.

The roar of the gun punctuated the stillness.

"Dear God!" Marie sobbed.

Still John stood. "Have mercy. Please, have mercy," his voice rang out.

"Ha-a-ave mer-r-rcy. Please, have mer-r-r-rcy." The hills echoed mockingly. "Have mer-r-r-r-r-rcy."

The gunman was only 20 feet from John. Why wasn't he hitting his target? The threads of hope continued to weave themselves in Marie's heart. Surely it was a game to frighten them. If it was, it surely had accomplished its purpose. "Please, dear God, let them stop!"

The gunman leveled his gun and then lowered it. He turned toward his partner with a look that said, "I can't do it!"

Indignantly, the commander raised his gun and stepped toward John. John hunched his shoulders and turned to the side as if to shield himself from the bullet. As the gunman squeezed the trigger, flames exploded from the gun barrel. The prayer died on John's lips as he slumped to the ground and lay still.

4

Blood and Tears

"Jo-h-h-hn!" Marie cried. Her voice was weak and strangled. The children whimpered and clung to her, their eyes wide with horror.

In a quick motion, the terrorist pivoted and fired at Gary. A searing pain ripped through his chest as he allowed the impact of the bullet to throw his body backwards. *Let them think I'm dead,* he thought as he crumpled to the ground.

Lying with his face in the cold damp grass, Gary tensed for another bullet that would tear through him any minute. "Lie still," he told himself. "Don't move or they'll see that you aren't dead yet."

As he waited for the shot to come, he thought, *So this is what it feels like to die.* Scenes from his life flashed in front of his eyes.

"Into thy hands I commend my spirit," he prayed silently, repeating the words of One who too had been "killed" by those He came to help.

Fear surged over him. The terrorists had intended to kill him. Were they watching from the shadows to send a final bullet through his chest at any sign of life?

Across the mountains and into the night echoed an agonized, heart-rending cry. "Joh-h-h-h-h-h-hn!"

"Joh-h-hn!" Marie sobbed as she ran to the silent, prostrate form of her husband. He lay very still, his breath coming in jerky gasps.

The terrorists sauntered up the trail and vanished into the night.

"Gary!" a voice hissed. "Gary!" But he lay still.

The padding of footsteps approached him. He tensed and held his breath, trying to look dead. A face bent over him. Then he could hear the footsteps fading away. Slowly he lifted one eyelid. He saw only Emiliana's retreating figure.

"Emiliana!" he whispered. "Have they gone yet?"

"Yes," she replied, "they've gone. I thought you were dead."

Painfully he pulled himself up and looked around. John was lying very still. Marie was bending over him, sobbing, "Don't die, John. Please don't die. You have five children to live for. Can you hear me? Wiggle your fingers so I know you can hear me. Don't die, John!" But he did not respond.

Marie examined her husband with the expertise of a nurse as she pled with him to live. Blood gushed from his shredded arm like water from a faucet, soaking the ground beneath him as she tried to stop the flow with her hand.

"He's bleeding very badly," she told Gary as he dragged himself over to them.

Gary handed his bloody shirt to Marie. "Use it for a tourniquet," he instructed, collapsing on the ground.

The children slipped up beside their mother and huddled beside their father's unconscious body. Their eyes were wide in horror as they whimpered, "Daddy! Daddy!"

Lovingly, Marie secured the tourniquet, then held her face to John's lips to listen for his breathing. She held her fingers to his wrist waiting for a pulse . . . waiting, praying, hoping, crying. . . .

A little hand tugged at her sleeve. Putting her arms about Timothy, John Ray, and Marilyn, Marie drew them to herself and held them close. Her tears dripped on their little heads.

"Daddy is going to be with Jesus," she whispered. "Would you like to kiss him good-bye?"

Three small pairs of lips touched the white cheeks and a flood of tears bathed the still face. Tears coursing down his cheeks, Gary turned his face from the scene. "O God! Why couldn't it have been me instead of John?"

Marie worked tenderly, urgently over the

body of her dearest though her fingers felt no pulse. She continued to hope desperately that he was only in shock. The tourniquet had slowed the bleeding of his arm. Surely he would revive soon. With all her heart she yearned for the still body to revive. In the darkness she could not see that he had other wounds.

The only sounds were the far-off bray of a donkey answered by the startled crow of a rooster.

Finally, she turned to Gary. Her voice was soft. "I'm afraid he's gone. He's just sleeping so peacefully."

"I'm sorry, Marie." Gary's voice was husky. *I'd give my life to remove the anguish in her eyes,* he thought to himself.

The young mother gathered her three oldest children into her lap as the twins slept on a blanket beside her. She stared mutely into the darkness, stroking the soft hair of her small sons as the tears flowed down her cheeks and dripped onto their heads. The realization of what had taken place rushed over her like an avalanche from which she could not escape. She could not feel the cool breeze nor hear the distant barking of a dog. She could not see the majestic mountains etched against the inky sky below the twinkling stars. She could only see the form that slept too peacefully and smell the lingering scent of gunpowder and feel the damp blood on her fingers.

"Daddy wake up soon?" Timothy wondered tugging at her sleeve.

"He woke up in heaven, dear." Her voice was a mere whisper.

"When will he come back to us?" John Ray asked, his face puzzled and questioning as he gazed at his father.

"He is waiting in heaven for us to come to him." Marie brushed away the tears that escaped from her eyes. "If we love and obey God, someday He will take us to heaven to be with Daddy again."

"Me want my daddy now!" Timothy wailed.

"How can he be in heaven when we see him here?" Marilyn asked.

Marie held them close. "The part of Daddy that talks and sees and hears is in heaven. God will give him a new, better body and he doesn't need this one anymore. You'll need to be Mommy's helpers now that Daddy isn't here to help me anymore."

"Those men that shot my daddy are mean."

"When I get big, I'll shoot the bad men that killed Daddy."

"Children," Marie sighed and drew them close. "Even if Daddy would have had ten guns in the house, he wouldn't have shot those men, and he wouldn't want you to either. We must love those men. Daddy would want us to love

41

them and pray for them."

Marie continued to reassure and hold the children close while the twins slept on. Before long, the little heads began to droop.

5

Smoke and Fog

Marie stared silently at the flames still leaping from the burning shed and Blazer. Suddenly, she knew what she must do. Laying the sleeping children onto a blanket on the ground, she turned to Gary who lay shivering in the wet grass. "I'm going to the house for a minute. I've got to get the passports."

Gary drew himself up on one elbow. "No, Marie! You daren't. It'll go up in flames any second. It's saturated with fuel. It'll explode! You can't go!"

"That's exactly why I've got to go before the passports go up in smoke. Who knows how long it'll take to get out of the country if that happens. Besides, you need a blanket, Gary. I've got to go," she spoke with a calm, determined voice.

"You could be killed, Marie!"

"I'll hurry. Emiliana, come help me. Please watch the children, Gary."

"Marie—" It was useless to argue. Marie was already running up the path. *What a brave girl,* he thought. *She's got her head together even though her world has just been blown to bits.*

Smoke rose from the shed. Flames still licked at the skeleton of the gutted Blazer. The hood of the Blazer hung cock-eyed, propped open on one side. The driver's door stood open, revealing coils of springs where the seat had been. As the women approached the house, smoke surrounded them, stinging their eyes and causing them to cough.

The door of the house stood ajar. Marie and Emiliana crept inside. The overpowering smell of kerosene mingled with smoke and stung their eyes and nostrils. Marie groped through the debris-strewn house, sloshing through pools of kerosene and crunching over shards of broken glass.

The only light to guide their way was the glow from the flames that shone through the windows. Shadows quivered against the pale walls.

Every footstep echoed the hollow emptiness that ached within her heart.

Marie stood surveying the smashed dishes and overturned furniture littering the floor, and the disemboweled drawers and cupboards. An overwhelming sense of invasion swept over her. Her private life had been invaded, plundered, rummaged through by greasy fingers, and trampled over by muddy boots. The stinging smoke smell mingling with the fumes of kerosene reminded her to hurry. This was no time to be overwhelmed.

Stumbling across overturned drawers, Marie found the open file drawers. She felt through the folders for the thin packet of passports. "Here they are! Thank You, God."

As Marie entered the bedroom, she saw a pair of mud-covered, worn-out shoes looking starkly out of place as they stood where John's had been.

In the pale, flickering light, Marie found John's white shirt and his suit. He would need them, yes, even if he wore them only to be buried in. She touched the soft lining. The faint scent of cologne drifted up to her nostrils, triggering a hundred memories—memories of her wedding day, memories of voices singing "God's Way Is Best." The memories stabbed her heart. Burying her face in the rough fabric, she wept for the arms to fill the sleeves again. "Oh God, I can't bear this."

Again the strong smell of smoke and the memory of Gary's words, "It could explode any minute," prodded her to hurry. Grabbing her navy dress from the hanger, she rummaged through piles of scattered clothing dumped onto the floor in the children's room. She selected a set of clothing for each of the little ones.

Quickly—let me think—we have the blankets.

Is there anything else we need urgently? Oh, the photo albums. It'll make it easier to face the future if I have the comfort of those memories.

"Let's go, Emiliana. That's all there is time for."

Arms laden, the two felt their way through the clutter to the open door.

Marie glanced at the charred metal that had once been the Blazer. The flames burned lower in the gutted vehicle. "If the house hasn't gone yet, it may not go," she remarked to Emiliana.

Gary saw them come. "Thank God," he whispered. "I sure didn't want to be left alone and bleeding on this mountain with five orphans."

Marie covered Gary with a blanket and tenderly arranged one over John's still body. "Oh John!" her heart cried out in fresh anguish as she knelt on the ground beside him, holding his wrist, waiting for the pulse that wouldn't throb. Tears poured down her cheeks again. "John!"

For several long moments there were only the night noises—the mournful call of a bird, a distant drunken laugh, and the sighing of the wind in the pines.

As Gary stared into the shadows, he was aware that those who had tried to murder him could be lingering in the thick undergrowth, watching for any sign of life. He pulled himself to a sitting position.

"Marie, have you thought of the fact that they could come back? I think we should walk over to

Pablo's house. At least there we'd be out of sight, and we could warm ourselves by the fire."

Marie looked up at him. Her brown eyes were pools of grief. "I can't bear to leave him, Gary, as long as there is any hope at all. I just can't. You go. It's you they want. They won't hurt me, and besides, you'll soon go into shock if you don't have the warmth of a fire."

"Marie, I can't leave you alone like this!"

"What could you do if they did come back? We'll be all right. Please go. I couldn't bear it if you went into shock and would die too." Her voice faded away.

Gary hesitated. How could he leave her alone and unprotected? Yet she was right. What could he do? What had he been able to do when they had been here before?

Sensing Marie's need to be alone, he hobbled to Pablo's, leaning on John Ray for support, breathing a prayer for Marie as he went. Each step sent fresh stabs of pain through his chest.

Marie sat as if she were a carving, sculptured out of the mountain, motionless, gazing sightlessly across the valley and into the black night. A damp mist settled over the mountain, winding its heavy shroud over the ridges and knolls. The stars flickered out like tiny flames of a hundred candles blown out in the breeze.

Shivering, Marie pulled a blanket around her. She drew herself within its roomy darkness like a caterpillar within its cocoon, longing to escape the reality of the silent form beside her. It seemed as though her life had become like the empty bullet cartridge that lay at her feet, like the shattered dishes that lay on the floor of the house.

She buried her face in the rough fabric of John's coat. "Johhhn," she wept. The sobs pushed from her heart in a torrent of tears.

"O God!" she cried. "You'll have to be my strength and hold me up. I've no one to lean on but You. Help me be brave for the children. The future, Lord! I have no house, no car, and almost no money."

The cry of a bird overhead drew to her memory the verse, "Are not five sparrows sold for two farthings, and not one of them is forgotten before God? But even the very hairs of your head are all numbered. Fear not therefore: ye are of more value than many sparrows" (Luke 12:6, 7).

Thinking of the mountains all around her, Marie's mind went to the Scripture. "I will lift up mine eyes unto the hills, from whence cometh my help. My help cometh from the LORD" (Psalm 121:1, 2).

"And we know that all things work together for good to them that love God, to them who are the called according to his purpose" (Romans 8:28). The verses poured over her heart like healing ointment. *We are called . . . He must have a purpose . . . but what? O Lord, show me!*

"If I would give you a glimpse of the future," God seemed to say, "you would see that your future will work out far better than you could imagine."

Though Marie felt alone and longed to be held and comforted, yet she drew strength from these quiet moments of meditation and reminiscing as she waited for dawn to break and end the long night.

When Gary arrived at Pablo's house, weak from exertion and loss of blood, the door stood ajar and the house was empty. Wrapping himself in his blanket, he lay on the dirt floor near the glowing embers and waited.

Before long, Pablo's family returned from the cornfield where they had hidden at the first sounds of gunfire. "I'll go for help," Pablo said bravely. But Pablo could not convince anyone to go with him while the assassins were at large on the dark mountain.

Gary could not rest as he thought of Marie weeping alone in the cold night. "Please tell Marie to come. Tell her I'll rest better if she and the children are here."

So Marie came. The children nestled down and soon feel into an exhausted slumber. But every time Marie closed her eyes, she saw the flash of gunfire and the still form of her husband.

Again the verses came. "And we know that all things work together for good to them that love God, to them who are the called according to his purpose."

Her eyes rested on Gary. He was lying too still. She could not hear him breathe. She reached for his wrist in the darkness. Thank God, he still had a faint pulse. His breath came soft and jerky, but he was still breathing. Though he was helpless to defend her and too weak to talk much, his very presence was a comfort to her.

"Gary's lost a lot of blood," Marie whispered to Pablo's wife. "He's got to have water." Between the sips of water Marie poured between Gary's lips, she talked to him to keep him conscious.

There were footsteps outside the house. Marie drew back in apprehension. The door opened and a dark face peered inside. She released her breath when she recognized the youth to be a friend of Gary's.

"We've come to see Gary," he began hesitantly. "We were so sad to hear what happened." Two other heads peered over his shoulder.

"Come in," Marie invited. "He's too weak to talk much, but I'm sure he'd be glad to see you."

Eyes wide, the three crept timidly to Gary's side. "How are you doing?" one questioned quietly.

Gary turned his head and opened his eyes.

"It's better now," he whispered feebly.

"Shall we pray?"

"Please."

The three knelt at Gary's side. Tears streamed down their faces as they prayed earnestly in the Cakchiquel dialect. Though Gary could not understand their words, he felt their anguish and wept with them.

"Faithfully follow God, and we will meet in eternity if we never see each other here again," Gary whispered as they rose to leave.

As Marie sipped coffee Pablo's wife had served her and waited for morning to come, she kept thinking, *What if John revives and needs me?*

"I'd like to walk over to John and see if perhaps there is any life at all," Marie said softly to Pablo's wife who sat near in silent grief.

Pablo's wife rose stiffly. "I'll go with you."

In the heavy darkness of the fog-shrouded night, Marie could not see the blanketed form until she was almost upon it. She knelt beside her husband. His face held a look of peace. Marie laid her hand on John's pale cheek. It was cold to her touch. For several seconds she knelt in utter silence. A dark hole, far darker than any night could ever be, opened within her heart as she realized those strong arms would never cradle her babies again. "Oh John dear, it hurts so to let you go."

6

Rescue

As the blood of dawn oozed across the sky, a lone figure flitted over the ridges. Like a bird, Pablo flew from rock to rock, tears blinding his eyes as urgency pressed him onward. Brother Gary was bleeding. Perhaps he too would die if help could not be reached soon.

It was 6:45 when Bill Byler hurried to answer the urgent pounding at the front door of the mission house in Chimaltenango. Opening the door, he was startled by the wild look on the frightened face of Pablo.

"They have shot and killed John!" Pablo burst out.

Bill staggered back a step as if he had been slapped across the face. He grasped the door frame for support. "What do you mean, they have shot and killed John?"

"Yes," Pablo insisted, his dark eyes wide. "They came in and tore up the house and killed

John!"

Stumbling into the bedroom, Bill half whispered, "Judy, Pablo Cortez is here, and he says John has been killed."

He stared unseeingly at his infant daughter sleeping in her crib, thinking of the two fatherless babies at Palamá.

"I've got to go tell the others at Headquarters."

When Bill and Pablo burst into the mission headquarters, the other missionaries were eating breakfast around the kitchen table, discussing the plans for the day. The missionaries from all stations under Conservative Mennonite Missions had planned to help on a building project at El Rodeo, where the Vernon Miller family and Sharon Knepp were stationed. John Troyer's family was expected to arrive soon, as well as Merle Yoders, who were stationed at Las Lomas.

"Good morning, Bill!" Dale Point called cheerfully. "How are you doing?"

"I'm—" Bill began, as he staggered to the counter, his face ashen, his hand clutching his chest. He leaned against the cupboard and covered his face with his hand.

Dale shoved back his chair and ran to Bill's side. He grabbed Bill's arm and shook him. "Bill! What's wrong? What's the matter?"

With tormented eyes, Bill turned to the group. "They've—they've shot and killed John."

The women gasped in horror.

"Shot and killed John?" Dale shouted. "What do you mean?"

"I don't know, but Pablo is here and he says they killed John and wounded Gary. They've torn up the house, and Marie's back there all alone with the children. What are we going to do?" he cried as he paced the floor. "We've got to let Merle know!"

Hurrying to the radio, the men called Vernon Millers and Merle Yoders. "Come to Headquarters immediately and bring your families," they were told. The nature of the emergency was not mentioned due to the stolen radios at large. Merle's wife answered the call at Las Lomas. "Merle is already on his way to Chimaltenango," she told them.

"We have to wait for Merle," Bill decided.

"No!" Dale was emphatic. "We can't wait! Get on the cycle and go! Take Davey with you, and get back there. Somebody's got to get back there for Marie's sake!

"You and Davey are the two best cyclists," Dale continued. "A cycle can get back there quicker than a truck. I'll stay here and organize the rescue."

In a daze, Bill grabbed his cycle gear, and he and David Yoder hopped on their cycles.

"We'll send a Blazer in for Gary," Dale called after them.

Stopping at his house, Bill told his wife he was going back to Palamá.

"Oh, Bill!" Judy cried. "You could get shot, too!"

"If you were back there alone, I'd want someone to go help you. I've got to go."

Only days before, shots had exploded outside the barn where Bill had been working. Fearing the shots were meant for him, he had switched off the lights and hidden. Later, he found that a neighbor woman and her daughter had been killed while the father escaped from those who had come to settle a grudge.

The two cycles sped over the Pan American Highway for 20 miles, threading in and out around ox carts, bicycles, and crowded, rattling buses. After driving through the town of Tecpan, the cycles skidded to a stop, their tires spewing gravel. Ahead of them, the road was blocked with felled trees, piles of rocks, scattered nails, and broken telephone poles. But roadblocks would not keep them from reaching Palamá. The cycles bounced through ditches the last mile and a half before they turned off onto the rutted road to Palamá.

What a blessing it is that the road is dry! Bill thought to himself. This was September, the rainiest month of the year. At times the mud made the road totally impassable. Other times it could take as long as seven hours to travel the eight miles. Occasionally, a winch was needed besides chains on the wheels of a four-wheel-drive vehicle. "Thank You, God," he whispered as he leaned into a sharp curve that dropped off into space.

As they neared Palamá, Bill gunned his cycle and cut through the woods on a narrow footpath. He didn't take time to think of the guerillas that could be waiting to ambush him on this lonely trail.

Cresting a knoll, Bill saw the gutted remains of the Blazer. Over 200 people crowded on the banks above the house, spilling down around the sides and sitting in the lawn below the house, watching, weeping quietly, and talking in undertones. Then he saw the still, blanketed form. It was true.

Lifting his eyes, he saw Marie walking slowly toward him, three little ones at her side and a whimpering baby in her arms.

"Marie!" he cried. "I can't believe it. Is it true? I can't believe it!"

Her sad voice was soft and controlled. "It is true, Bill."

Looking down at John Ray, Marilyn, and Timothy, Bill recalled his own father's death when he was five. All the frustration he felt as a small boy standing beside his father's casket poured over his soul. "You dear children!" his heart cried as he fell on his knees, wrapped his arms around the little ones, and wept with them.

* * * * *

Back at Chimaltenango, Merle Yoder was met with the sad news when he drove into Headquarters with his Blazer. He turned to the others, his shoulders bent with the weight of sorrow. "I'll go back and bring Gary out to the hospital," he offered.

"We should send some women to comfort Marie and to help her pack," someone suggested. Judy Byler and Phyllis Bear climbed into the Blazer with Merle and Pablo.

* * * * *

Lying in Pablo's house back at Palamá, Gary was growing weaker. "He must have help now," the villagers decided. "We can't wait for the mission vehicle to get here."

A licensed villager and an old pickup were located. The seat of the truck was removed and replaced by a mattress.

* * * * *

As David's cycle soared over the last ridge, the cloudless sky spread out before him. It was hard to believe that the remains of a tragedy awaited him around the curve on such a lovely day. As he rounded the curve, he saw the crowds of people.

He pressed past the crowd. *I've got to find*

Gary! David thought, not knowing whether his friend was alive or dead. He remembered hearing someone say Gary had gone to Pablo's house.

As he sped toward Pablo's house, a battered pickup rumbled toward him and slowed to a stop. Gary lay silently on the mattress. David sighed in relief when Gary turned to look at him. *He's still alive!* David thought. *I'll ride along to make sure he gets to the hospital as soon as possible.*

* * * * *

After listening to Marie's story, Bill heard the rattle of the old pickup. Turning, he saw the truck with Gary in it.

"I hate to leave Marie," Gary murmured from his mattress as Bill leaned in the window to talk to him. Having shared the horror of the night with Marie and the children and knowing the trauma they had experienced, he wanted to be supportive and ease the pain in any way he could.

"Gary," Bill told him firmly, "you are going to have to go. We are here now and others are coming. You need to take care of yourself. We'll be praying for you."

The pickup truck bounced over the ridges, leaving a trail of dust and squawking chickens. Every bump was torture for Gary, sending fresh pain through his chest. He gritted his teeth as the rutted trail threw him from one side of the pickup to the other.

Meanwhile, Merle was headed down the mountain road, negotiating the curves with urgent, record-breaking speed. When his Blazer careened around a curve, the pickup veered off the road and lurched to a stop in a cloud of dust. Gently Gary was transferred to the mission Blazer. Merle grew pale when he saw Gary's bloody clothing and colorless face. "He seems awfully weak," Merle worried.

"We'll walk the last half mile," Judy told Merle. "You just get Gary to the hospital before it's too late for him."

Holding down the accelerator as far as he dared and racing back the way he had just come, Merle guided the vehicle away from the largest ruts and rocks, blowing his horn to clear the trail of dogs, chickens, and children. He swerved around blockades of felled trees and rocks. Nails and tacks carpeted the road, stabbing the tires. Yet the vehicle sped on.

There has got to be a mistake! Merle kept thinking. *John, so full of life, so needed by his church and family, cannot be dead.* But when he looked at the blood on Gary, he knew it was true. Working with John the last several years had forged a close friendship between the two. He felt almost as though a part of his heart had been ripped from his chest and lay bleeding and dead

The John Troyer family in 1981.

The Troyer house and Blazer following the attack.

The door scarred with machete slash marks and bullet holes.

The still blanketed form.

The gutted Blazer with John Ray in the foreground wearing his father's brown hat.

Waiting for the *alcalde*.

Emiliana with Marilyn.

John (in the right foreground) as his fellow workers remembered him.

Guatemalans singing Bienvenido.

Missionary Pastor Slain
In Guatemala;

Misionero USA asesinado ayer

The Miami Herald / International Ed
Friday, September 18, 1981

American missionary is slain in Guatemala

GUATEMALA CITY — Terrorists shouting anti-American slogans ransack
ary's h
death in
children.
sionary w
A U.S.
nesday
American

By STEVE BELL
Times Writer

FAIRVIEW — Murdered by terror-
nno-
was
't of
nple

I have fought a good fight, I have finished my
course, I have kept the faith   II Tim. 4:7

Guatamalan terrorists

800 honor slain missionary

Jose Patzan, 28, a Guatemalan native attending the funeral, said it was hard to say why his countrymen would choose to kill a man like Troyer.

"He was a good brother in our place," said Patzan, a member of the mission board along with Troyer. "He was trying to help Guatemala."

You've hastened on, now, John,
And cannot to the harvest go.
You labored well; the grain was coming in,
And help was on the way. But no —
God called, and suddenly you're gone,
Snatched from the fields you dearly loved,
To sweet and well-earned rest with Him.

IN MEMORY OF
John David Troyer
1953-1981

THE INDIANAPOLIS STAR   1971.

The relatives said Troyer of Fairview, Mich., had lived in Guatemala seven years, advising local farmers and agricultural cooperatives on improving their crops and farming methods

Mrs. Troyer told relatives that terrorists came to their home before dawn Sunday and gunned down her husband as she and the children looked on.

Sturgis Journal, Saturday, September 19, 1981

A U.S. Embassy spokesman said about 10 gunmen, shouting anti-American slogans, burst into Troyer's home and herded Troyer, his wife, their five children and another missionary outside the house at gunpoint.

The gunmen ransacked the house, set fire to the mission's truck and then opened fire on the two men, the spokesman said.

The other missionary, Gary Miller, 21, of Norfolk, Va., was in satisfactory condition after being seriously wounded in the chest during the attack.

John David Troyer, the Conservative Mennonite Fellowship missionary slain in September in Guatemala, was in prayer at the moment of his death.

Terrorists shoot

Area Man Shot In Guatemala

A Hyde County man who was working in Guatemala as a Mennonite mission has been shot, the Daily News has learned.

Gary L. Miller, 21, son of Mr. and Mrs. Marion Miller, of the Grassy Ridge community, is being treated for a gunshot wound in the hospital in Guate...

Guatemala shooting

there.

An hour later, Troyer's car and power generator were burned. Troyer was dead and Miller...

Miller said that he would return to Guatemala and continue his work as a missionary if the conditions were safe and stable, and if he felt that God was calling him to return to that country.

But all that chan... hours of Monda...

"It w...

Miller said that he and the Troyers were unarmed. "Even if we had had ten guns in the house we wouldn't have used them," said Miller.

...way to the ...nem and notified

Misionero menoni asesinado en Tec

El misionero norteamericano, David Troyer, de la orden...

"The terrorism in Guatemala will not prevail against the church," said Bear. "The church will go on."

Bear, who had spoken with Troyer when he first asked to perform missionary work in 1972, was unable to complete his sermon uninterrupted as he joined men and women in the audience in tears.

"The concern he had for souls — not only for himself, but for others — is going to live on," Bear said. "I'm convinced that even in his death, much more will be accomplished yet.

"The blood of martyrs is the seed of the church."

RICHARD VAN NOSTRAND

The widow of John Troyer, Marie, and her four-year-old daughter, Marilyn, walk to the gravesite, escorted by David Gordon, director of Gordon's Funeral Home of Mio.

The Gary Miller family in 1991.
Row 3: Gary and Marie
Row 2: John Ray, Marilyn, Timothy
Row 1: Sharon, Christopher, Karen, Jessica

beside John's body.

* * * * *

At the headquarters in Chimaltenango, Guatemalan and missionary youth girls gathered in a bedroom, praying for Gary and for the family back at Palamá. Their hands were joined as they stood in a circle, crying and praying. Hearing the Blazer pull through the mission gate, they ran outside to watch as the mattress beneath Gary was gently lifted from the Blazer, and eased into the mission van. Gary was bloody, dirty, moaning softly, and growing weaker.

"I'll take the Blazer to Las Lomas to pick up your family!" Dale called as Merle jumped into the driver's seat of the mission van. Nails from the roadblocks had punctured the Blazer's tires, but none had deflated. The tires continued to hold their air until Dale returned safely with Merle's family. Only then did the tires go flat, although one tire held eight nails.

Zipping in and out of traffic, the lights of the van flashed and the horn shrieked as Merle raced to the hospital in Guatemala City.

David sat at Gary's side, praying and trying to keep his friend as comfortable as possible. At the hospital, he stayed with Gary while Merle drove on to inform the American Embassy of the murder.

The sun continued to rise in the sky. Back at

Palamá, Bill told the Indians standing around the blanketed body, "We've got to move John to shade inside the church."

"You can't!" they replied. "You'll get into trouble if you do! It's illegal to touch a murder victim until the *alcalde* (ahl CAHL day) comes. But we'll help you build a shelter." So a crude shelter was constructed from saplings and scrap sheets of tin.

Judy and Phyllis threw their arms around Marie and wept with her. After they dried their tears, the women surveyed the clutter about them. "Let us help you pack up," they told Marie. "You'll want to get out of here before dark."

Marie remained collected as she decided what Judy and Phyllis should pack. The women raced with the sun, stuffing fuel-soaked clothing that they sorted from the clutter into dresser drawers. They would not be found here at night when the terrorists might return to finish their work.

As Marie picked up her belongings from the floor where they had been dumped and rooted through, she felt for a moment as though someone had reached inside her heart, crushed it, and taken what was dearest to her, leaving her empty and shattered. Was it only last night that this home had sheltered a happy family? Was it only last night that John sat on his chair by the hearth?

As Marie packed away the newborn baby clothing, she thought, *I won't need these anymore. I'll never get married again.*

The babies were getting fussy despite Emiliana's best efforts to keep them happy. "I can't find Karen's pacifier," Marie told Bill. "I think—John may have had it in his pocket. Would—would you mind checking?"

Bill searched through each pocket, but he could not find the missing pacifier. Instead he found a bullet wound in John's leg, two in his shoulder blade and the wound that shredded his arm. He could not see the hole at the back of John's head.

Inside the house, Bill noticed that the pilot light of the stove was lit, while pools of fuel still lay everywhere. Bill quickly extinguished the flame, wondering what had kept the house from exploding. Checking around the back of the house, he found the wood siding blistered. The coals still smouldered from what had been the woodpile, ten feet away. *Why didn't the house burn?* he asked himself. But in his heart he knew.

God must have kept the Blazer from exploding, he thought, studying the gutted remains of the vehicle that lay only several feet from the porch. *If the Blazer would have exploded, the house would surely have gone, like the terrorists had planned.*

"The children are getting hungry," Marie remarked to the women. "I don't know if we can find anything fit to eat with all the fuel that was splashed over everything."

"Here are some eggs some of the villagers brought," one of the women replied. "It's too dangerous to light a fire in the stove with all the fuel lying around, but maybe we can cook them over the coals left from last night's fire." So the meal consisted of eggs cooked over the coals from the remains of the woodpile, along with baked goods Marie had prepared on Saturday.

A small pickup roared up the mountain like a tornado. Seven men armed with machine guns leaped from the truck bed and took positions in a circle around John's body, their guns poised.

The guerillas have come back to get us all! Bill thought in horror.

"It's the *alcalde*," the villagers murmured, stepping back respectfully for the mayor of Tecpan.

After a few brief questions from the official Merle had notified, John's body was wrapped and lifted onto the pickup bed. The armed men jumped on, and the truck sped down the mountain as if to outrace any guerillas that might be lurking behind the rocks. The *alcalde* would take the body to Tecpan where papers needed to be filled out and a hearse would be waiting.

Vernon Miller left Chimaltenango, wanting to

assist the family back at Palamá. He had grown up with John and felt the loss keenly. Punctured tires from the scattered nails around the road-blocks, however, forced him to turn back to Chimaltenango.

Lester Martin and John Point, V.S. workers from Chimaltenango, arrived at Palamá with two vehicles, each pulling a small trailer. Dressers and boxes were carried from the house and loaded onto the trailers.

Thinking of the guerillas that could be waiting to ambush the vehicles as they wound down the lonely mountainside, John Point offered to take Bill's cycle back to Headquarters for him. "I'll take the footpath since the guerillas would likely be waiting for the vehicles on the other road," the teenager planned.

"That will work out fine," Bill replied. "Some-one needs to take the mayor's assistant to Tecpan to sign the papers anyway. You'd better start now. You'll have to bring him back again."

"Uh, sure," John gulped. He hadn't counted on that. The mayor's assistant climbed on the cycle behind John, and the two headed down the trail.

As news flashed across the mountainside, weeping Indians continued to stream toward the mission house. Between three and four hundred friends pressed about Marie, embracing her, weeping. "John was our brother. We loved him.

He helped us so much. We are so sorry for what happened. We'll never forget the testimony he gave last night. 'For me to live is Christ, and to die is gain.'"

As the last box was loaded into the trailer, Marie was encouraging the people that crowded around her. "Stay faithful no matter what happens. All the trials we face in this life will be forgotten when we see Jesus."

"Marie," Bill called. "We need to leave right away. We are going to get caught on the trail after dark if we don't go now."

Leaving part of her heart with the crowd that stood weeping and waving on the hillside, Marie lifted the children into the Blazer. Emiliana climbed in after her with one of the twins.

Tear-stained faces pressed near the windows. *"Adios! Adios! Adios!"* they cried. "Good-bye!"

As the procession pulled away from the weeping crowd waving a last farewell, the tears of hundreds of Indians bore witness to the tragedy of the previous night. Doleful, deserted expressions pinched their faces. "What will we do now?" they murmured to each other. "What will we do without John?"

Word spread ahead of the little caravan that wound its way down the mountain. Sad-faced Indians stood along the road to wave a teary farewell.

Tears slid down Marie's cheeks as she waved

out the window. Tears, not for her own sorrow, but for grief of the ones who were left behind to find their way without their shepherd.

As the vehicles neared the main highway, they met John Point and the mayor's assistant, starting back up the dirt road. "Oh, no," Point groaned to himself. "I'm going to be the last one out."

When the procession of vehicles and trailers reached the highway, a mission Blazer waited with extra tires in case of flats due to the strewn nails. The two vehicles with the trailers were taken on to Chimaltenango. In the Blazer, Bill and Judy took Marie and her family to Tecpan, where papers needed to be signed before the hearse could take the body to the city for embalming. The American ambassador, with his entourage of cars, waited to talk with Marie.

"I'd like you to ride with me in my car to Chimaltenango," he told her. "I'd like to have you tell me what happened." An armed vehicle led the way, followed by the ambassador's car, then the mission Blazer, with another armed vehicle bringing up the rear. Darkness settled over them as they traveled the last 20 miles.

"I'll order an investigation," the ambassador assured Marie. She knew, however, that it was unlikely that the truth would be uncovered with the political turmoil the country was in. Yet Marie felt sure that it would not have been

justice that John would have wanted but forgiveness and salvation for those who had killed
him.

7

Till We Meet Again

At the mission headquarters in Chimal-tenango, Marie and her children were taken into the arms of the waiting missionary women.

As Marie bathed the twins, Dale held Timothy in his lap, reading him a story. "Bad mans killed me daddy. Bang!" the little fellow told Dale. "'Em go to 'ell."

"Now Timmy," Marie chided gently, having overheard from the bathroom. "We must pray for those men." How often she had repeated those words to the children. Yet it was good therapy for her, helping to turn the seeds of bitterness into feelings of compassion.

"Me have to drive the car now," Timothy told Dale.

"What? You have to drive the car?" Dale questioned. "Why do you have to do that?"

"Daddy can't drive car anymore, so me have to."

He understands more than we thought, Dale said to himself.

Surrounded with weeping fellow missionaries, Marie recalled the last workers' meeting that had been held at Headquarters several weeks before. She could hear John request the song "We have an anchor that keeps the soul / Steadfast and sure while the billows roll." Reminded that her heart was fastened to that anchor, Marie continued to function calmly in spite of the tears that often glistened in her eyes. Decisions faced her. Where should the funeral be held? Where should John be buried?

"I'd like to have a service held at Palamá," Marie told the others. "I just feel John would have wanted it. That was where his heart was."

"It's too dangerous," the mission board decided. "We cannot allow it. We can hold a memorial service in Chimaltenango, instead, if you wish."

"John and I had talked about the possibility of one of us dying here in Guatemala," Marie told the other missionaries. "We had decided if that were to happen, we'd let the parents of that person decide whether the body would be buried in Guatemala or taken back to the United States for burial. Maybe I should give Alvins a call and see what they think."

Sunday, Alvin and Luellen had spent an enjoyable day with friends at Traverse City, Michigan. While driving home Sunday night, the elder Troyers commented on the exceptionally bright light of the moon. They could easily have driven home without headlights.

Monday, John's mother Luellen had been working on peaches when she received a phone call from a mission board member. "Have you heard from John?" he had asked her. When she replied that she hadn't, he gently broke the sad news to her. Luellen was alone at the time and wept as she called her husband at the grocery store he operated. Alvin came home immediately, and the two of them cried together. "I'm so glad he called home Tuesday night," one of them remarked.

When Marie called them Monday night, the Troyers replied, "We'd like to have John's body brought home to Michigan for a funeral. There are those in the community whose lives could be touched by being at his funeral service. Yes, bring him home."

It was decided that following a viewing and memorial service at Chimaltenango, the casket, along with Marie's family, would be flown to the United States for a funeral and burial in John's hometown of Fairview, Michigan.

In Missouri, Marie's brother Levi Schrock and his wife drove to the hospital, where Marie's father was under care for heart problems, to tell their parents the sad news. Immediately,

Marie's mother and brother knew what they must do. They must go to Marie's side. Reservations were made for Levi and his mother to fly to Guatemala Tuesday morning.

* * * * *

It was nearly nine o'clock at Chimaltenango but John Point had not arrived at Headquarters yet. "Where is he?" his mother worried. "He should have been home hours ago. I hope he's okay."

Back on the road to Palamá, the sun had begun slipping behind the mountains when John felt the cycle tire squish beneath him. His fears were confirmed. A nail from the roadblock had punctured the tire. John walked to the nearest village. "I don't have any money on me," the teenager communicated to the villagers in his limited Spanish, "but if someone will take me back to Chimaltenango, my dad will be glad to pay you."

"I'll take you for *veinte quetzales*," a villager responded. John climbed on the truck and helped load the motorcycle. Before long, he saw the lights of the mission, welcome beacons in the darkness.

"Thank God he's safe!" John's mother breathed as she watched her son unload the cycle.

Late into the night, lights burned at the

mission headquarters while the women washed, rewashed, and sorted the drawers of clothing that reeked of kerosene. The tables and counters in the kitchen were covered with stacks of laundry—diapers, small dresses, and little shirts and pants.

Marie left the laundry to put the children to bed. There was much she needed to do, but her children needed her. After helping them to relax, she prayed with them and held them until they fell into an exhausted slumber.

Various missionaries tossed in their beds that night, tensing at every creak, wondering if they would be next on the list.

Tuesday morning, Dale and John Point drove back to Palamá for another load of furnishings and to tell the people about the funeral, arranging to have them picked up that afternoon.

"But we want John buried here," an old man said with tears running down his face. "He was one of us."

Recalling the Guatemalans' respect for elders, Dale gently explained, "John's father and grandfather are still alive, so they will decide." The villager seemed to understand.

When the undertaker unloaded the coffin at the mission headquarters, he asked, "Was this man a Christian?"

"He sure was," one of the missionaries replied.

"I could tell that he was," the undertaker stated. "His muscles were so relaxed. The muscles of a dead non-Christian are generally tense, while a Christian's muscles are relaxed. It is remarkable that Mr. Troyer's muscles were that relaxed, knowing his death came the way it did, facing the gun."

Marie walked into the chapel where the casket was standing. There was an element of permanence and foreboding in seeing the casket; yet Marie wanted to see John before the chapel filled with mourners. He was dressed in the white shirt and the suit she had carried out of the house two nights before. She could almost smell a whiff of kerosene.

John looked fairly natural. His face held a peaceful expression as his head rested on the soft pillow. "John dear," she said as she laid her hand on his cold cheek.

He is only asleep, she told herself as she blinked back the tears. *He'll wake up on that last morning.*

As she walked out of the dark chapel and into the bright sunlight, Marie saw Mark and Norma Gingerich walking toward her. The sight of them brought back memories of the happy months she had spent with them at Palamá, memories of the drone of John's cycle as he rode up the mountain to visit her when they were dating, memories of listening to "Dry Bones," a favorite recording of

John's—on their dates in Mark's living room.

Mark had taken Marie and John's engagement picture at the waterfalls below Palamá, where two rivers came together as one. The uniting of the rivers had been symbolic, but now there was only one river left to find its own way across the rocks.

"Norma!" the young widow cried as they fell into each other's arms.

"Marie!"

How soon plans can change, Mark thought as the two women wept together. Johns had planned to visit Marks at Guatemala City the night before, but now the Gingerichs had come to Marie instead.

"Please," Marie begged them. "Leave the country for your own safety's sake."

The benches in the chapel were filled with mourners. Chairs lined the walls. Yet the building could not hold all who came. Indians stood outside, clustered at the doorways and windows, straining to hear the music that floated out to them as the church youths sang.

Singing was difficult for the youths. They felt more like crying when they looked at the casket and the fatherless family. The notes drifted out the windows.

There's no disappointment in heaven,
No weariness, sorrow or pain,

No hearts that are bleeding and broken,
No song with a minor refrain.

The clouds of our earthly horizon
Will never appear in the sky,
For all will be sunshine and gladness,
With never a sob or a sigh.

I'm bound for that beautiful city
My Lord has prepared for His own.
Where all the redeemed of all ages
Sing "glory" around the white throne.

The room grew still as Bill rose to give a Spanish devotional meditation. He borrowed his theme from the sign in front of the nearby army camp: "Loyalty until death."

Struggling with deep feelings of loss, Merle Yoder wept as he spoke to the mourners. His sermon was centered around the theme, "God's ways and plans are above our ways." After Merle took his seat, native pastors and American missionaries rose to share tearful testimonies of appreciation for John Troyer.

After expressing how he had enjoyed working with John, Mark Gingerich shared a reading which reflected what John was experiencing.

"What must it be like to step on a shore—
     and to find it heaven,

To take hold of a hand—and to find it God's
hand,
To breathe a new air—and to find it celes-
tial air,
To feel invigorated—and to find it immor-
tality,
To rise from the care and turmoil of earth
into one unbroken calm,
To wake up—and to find it Glory?"
—Author Unknown

When the last person had shared his testimony
and the benediction had been pronounced, the
singing began again.

Safe in the arms of Jesus, Safe on His
gentle breast,
There by his love o'ershaded, Sweetly
my soul shall rest.
Hark! 'tis the voice of angels, Borne in a
song to me,
Over the fields of glory, Over the jasper
sea. . . .

Jesus, my heart's dear refuge, Jesus has
died for me;
Firm on the Rock of Ages, Ever my trust
shall be.
Here let me wait with patience, Wait till
the night is o'er;

Wait till I see the morning Break on the
golden shore.

Safe in the arms of Jesus, Safe on His
gentle breast,
There by His love o'ershaded, Sweetly
my soul shall rest.

As the young people sang, mourners filing past
the casket wept brokenly. *"Juan! Nuestro her-
mano Juan."* An Indian pastor tearfully kissed
the rigid face. *"Juan!"*

After lingering over the casket, the
Guatemalans turned to Marie who was seated on
the front bench with her two babies and three
children. Sobbing, the Indians embraced their
sister. Marie put her arms around them, whis-
pering words of comfort and hope.

Seeing the overflowing churchhouse, the
women preparing a meal added jugs of water to
stretch the huge pots of stew.

* * * * *

Marie's brother Levi and her mother Nettie
had arrived at the airport. On their way to
Chimaltenango, they stopped at the hospital to
see Gary. X-rays revealed that the bullet had not
lodged in his chest, but had exited through his
back. His wounds were cleaned and bandaged.
Gary had been kept *incognito* for safety's sake.

Unidentified individuals who asked for Gary Miller, could get no information that there even was such a patient at the hospital.

When Levi and Nettie arrived at Chimaltenango, Marie walked out to the yard to meet them. There she cried softly on the shoulders of her mother and brother.

That evening, Marie sat beside the casket, holding a baby, her children at her side. Hundreds of friends filed by, embracing her tearfully, murmuring words of sympathy, lingering mournfully over the body of their friend. They were heartbroken. They knew John had cared deeply for them, and they had loved him.

"Remain faithful," Marie encouraged them, tears shining in her eyes. "Look at this experience as a challenge, not a stumbling block. At least we know where John is. Many people have been kidnapped and tortured and are never heard from again, but we know John is not in the hands of torturers, but in heaven, where we'll see him again."

While weeping Indians poured into the mission house, Marie slipped away for a moment to comfort and pray with the children.

"We want our daddy!" the children sobbed.

"Daddy is in heaven where nothing can ever hurt him or make him sad again," Marie told them as she held them in her arms. While holding them close, she prayed for each that God would heal the hurt in their little hearts.

Marie returned to comfort and encourage the mourners that came. At 10:30, the line dwindled, yet sobbing Indians continued to knock on the door, asking to speak with Marie. Late into the night, Marie consoled the distraught mourners, though the final packing for the next day's flight to the States still waited to be completed. For the third night in a row, Marie slept very little. Nor would she get much more sleep before the week had ended.

All night long, a light burned in the mission chapel while Guatemalans from Chimaltenango and Palamá sat near the casket, silently, tearfully waiting for dawn, as was the custom of the country.

At daybreak, mourners came again to the mission compound to talk to Marie.

Guatemalans crowded into every spare inch of space in the vehicles taking Marie's family and her mother and brother to the airport. The final farewell would be postponed as long as possible.

After Marie had left, a call from the State Department of Guatemala came to the mission house at Chimaltenango, saying the President wished to express his condolences to Mrs. Troyer. But he was unable to speak to Marie, as she had already left the country.

Enroute to the airport, Marie stopped at the hospital to see Gary. "I brought the poem you wrote Sunday night," she told him, "I thought you would want it."

"Thanks," he told her, taking the poem. *She's one who is always reaching out to those around her,* Gary thought. *She must be a very selfless person to think of others in this time of deep grief.*

At the airport, boxes and suitcases were unloaded. After checking in the luggage, the group hurried to the point of departure. The boarding call for the flight to New Orleans had already been announced.

"We will not board the plane until we are certain the casket is loaded," Marie's brother Levi told the airport officials. He had been warned that they might arrive in the United States to find the casket was still in Guatemala. As John Point looked out the window, he could see a forklift loading the casket into the belly of the plane.

The Indians and missionaries stood in a circle around Marie. Tears streamed down their faces as they sang the Spanish words of "God Be With You Till We Meet Again."

"If we never meet here again, I'll meet you in the morning at the feet of Jesus," Marie told her weeping friends.

As Marie embraced Emiliana, she whispered, "Stay faithful, Emiliana. I'll write and wait to hear from you."

Waving a final farewell to her tearful friends she was leaving behind, Marie helped the children into the plane. *I never thought I'd leave this way*, she thought as she fastened the seat belts of the little ones and took a last look at the country she had learned to love.

She thought of the first time she had landed at this airport. John had been there to help her with the luggage. How different this flight would be.

As the plane lifted from the runway, the children punched the buttons on their uncle's musical calculator. Softly, it played the tune, "When the Saints Go Marching In."

8

Until the Golden Morning

After leaving the airport, the missionaries stopped at the hospital to pick up Gary. He had been released to fly to the States with the Vernon Miller family to attend John's funeral.

The bullet had passed through the tip of his lung and gone out his back. The lung had not collapsed, nor had it filled with blood. "If you were going to be shot," the doctor told him, "that was an ideal place for it to occur."

Skyscrapers, temple ruins, towering mountain peaks, and jade-colored jungle valleys passed beneath the plane. *Why?* Gary couldn't stop asking. *Why couldn't it have been me? John was a pastor. He had a family and a loving wife. Why was he killed instead of me?*

From the agony in his heart flowed the words of a poem.

God's Plan

God has a plan for everyone
That's in His service here,
A reason for his living now—
'Twill all one day be clear.

For earthly haze and finite mind
Obstruct from us the view
Of the purpose why God brings to us
Those dreary days and blue.

Why does a God of warmth and love
And tenderness and care
Lead sons of His through valleys dark
And cold and damp and bare?

Why does the God who loves us well
Allow the child of His
Experience bitter agony
Instead of purest bliss?

Why did our loving God allow
This sorrow in our lives,
When well we know He had the power
To let this bitter cup pass?

For in our feeble, human minds
We surely would have thought
A man like John had much to give
Of good, as yet unwrought.

But God said, "John, your time is up;
Come home and stay with Me.
Your time is finished down on earth;
Begun eternally.

Our God does not demand of us
To fully understand,
But meekly say, "Thy will be done,"
And follow in His plan.

And though the burden pressing down
Seems more than we can bear,
God's helping and sustaining grace
Will ceaselessly be there.

Some day a golden morn will dawn
And on that happy shore,
God's plan we'll fully understand,
And death will part no more.

Carefully Gary signed his name, folded his
poem, and tucked it into his shirt pocket. Tomorrow he would give it to Marie.

* * * * *

A solemn stillness shrouded the Fairview
Mennonite Church. Marie with her family followed the casket as it was carried into the
auditorium. Eight hundred sets of eyes turned
toward them in silent sympathy.

Dan Byler, a mission board member, rose to share a meditation. Having visited the Troyers at Palamá only a week before, Dan had told his wife, "If anyone is making a sacrifice, it is John, Marie, and Gary."

Opening his Bible to Revelation 14:13, Dan read, "Blessed are the dead which die in the Lord . . . henceforth . . . they may rest from their labours; and their works do follow them."

His eyes brimming with tears, the elderly pastor took his seat.

William Bear, a former fellow missionary of John's, began his sermon with verses 13 and 14 of I Thessalonians 4. "I would not have you to be ignorant, brethren, concerning them which are asleep, that ye sorrow not, even as others which have no hope. For if we believe that Jesus died and rose again, even so them also which sleep in Jesus will God bring with him."

"The book of the martyrs is opened again. We've heard the saying, 'The blood of the martyrs is the seed of the church.'

"The title for my message is 'A Life of Purpose.' I'm taking this from the words of our brother." William paused, fighting to gain control of his emotions. Wiping the tears that escaped from his eyes, he said brokenly, "I trust you'll bear with me if I break down a bit."

There was a moment of silence. All across the audience, women wiped their eyes and men blew their noses and cleared their throats while children sat like statues.

William pocketed his handkerchief. "In 1976, in the earthquake, God reached down and took 22,000 lives, most of them to eternal damnation." William's voice broke. "That is the tragic part. Most of them went to eternal damnation.

"When I returned to the states after the earthquake, I brought John and Marie and little John Ray with me.

"When John spoke at our home church, he said, 'Some thought Christ had come back that night of the great earthquake, and for 22,000 He had. But God spared me, and I believe he spared me for a purpose.'

"We believe that God did spare John for a purpose," William continued. "But we must trust that purpose has been fulfilled."

Marie dabbed at her eyes with a handkerchief. In her mind's eye she could see the 40-pound adobe block lying in John Ray's crib the night of the earthquake. She had taken John Ray to their bed hours before the quake when he had been unusually fussy. *God kept our family safe in a miraculous way that night, and I know He could have protected John Sunday night. His purpose must have been fulfilled.*

Turning to the sixteenth chaper of Luke, William told the story of the rich man and Lazarus. "Lazarus died and was carried by the angels to Abraham's bosom. I had to think of the morning . . . in the darkness, in the wee hours of the night as life ebbed out of our brother, the angels came and took the soul back to God who gave it. It says the rich man also died and was buried. In hell he lifted up his eyes, being in torment. He knew what the Law was, but he had not prepared.

"I have a quote here that John had written in his Bible," William continued. "'Life with Christ is an endless hope, but without Him it is a hopeless end.'"

After the benediction, soft strains of singing filled the church.

> When burdens come so hard to bear that
>   no earthly friend can share;
> Tears drive away the smiles and leave my
>   heart in pain.
> Then my Lord from heav'n above, speaks
>   to me in tones of love,
> Wipes the tears away and makes me
>   smile again.

Weeping friends filed by the open casket.

> I need no mansion here below for Jesus
>   said that I could go
> To a home beyond the clouds not made
>   with hands.

> Won't you come and go along? We will
>   sing the sweetest song
> Ever played upon the harps of glory
>   land.
>
> Oh, the tho't to me is sweet, that my
>   loved ones I will meet
> At the ending of the journey here below.
> Seems I hear their voices blend in a
>   world without an end;
> I won't worry when the time shall come
>   to go.

As the last notes faded away, a soothing balm poured over the young widow's aching heart. "Thank You, God. It helps me to cope, knowing I'll see John again."

With quiet composure, Marie led the children to the casket to view John's body a final time. John Ray stretched on tiptoe to peer over the edge of the metal casket while Marie lifted each child by turn for a last glimpse of their father's body.

She placed her hand on John's cold one. Tears glistening in her eyes, Marie gazed at each feature, painting them on the easel of her heart. For a long moment she forgot everything but the still face that rested on the silken pillow. Memories surged over her. Memories of being

stranded with John at the Guatemala airport . . .
memories of the nervousness of their first date at
Bible school . . . the wedding day . . . John's
ordination . . . the earthquake . . . the babies
. . . *Oh Johhhn!*

Sweet strains of music penetrated her
thoughts. It was the same song that had been
sung at their wedding seven years before.

> God's way is best; I will not murmur,
> Although the end I may not see;
> Where'er He leads I'll meekly follow—
> God's way is best, is best for me.

Marie held her handkerchief to her eyes for a
brief second, then calmly led her lambs to their
seats. The serenity that shone from her face,
radiated the assurance that the stormy clouds of
grief would evaporate into a golden dawn of a
new day when she would see John's face again.
The dawn would chase away the gloomy shadows
as the dawn that gilded the sky when Christ
arose to rend the dark veil of death's gloom. One
look upon the nail-scarred hands of Jesus, for
Whose cause her husband had given his life,
would take away all clouds of sorrow. It would be
worth it all!

9

All Things Work
Together for Good

Gary lay on the bed of his parents' camper as
they traveled home to North Carolina. His chest
throbbed painfully. Even more acute, however,
was the pain in his heart from the loss of his
friend and from thoughts of the fatherless home.

On Sunday, Gary's parents and brothers and
sisters gathered around him for a time of praying
and reading Scripture. Suddenly the feelings of
tension and grief that had been bottled within
him since the traumatic night one week before
uncorked. They gushed out in a torrent of tears.
"Why?" he cried. "Why couldn't it have been
me? What will happen with John's family? What
will become of his church?"

"You'll have to leave those questions with the
One who has the answers," Gary's father replied.

Gary knew it would be some time before the
wound in his chest would allow for the strenuous

work of hanging garage doors in his father's business. "Where do You want me now, Lord?" he prayed. "If the conditions stabilize, I'll return to Guatemala if You call me to go. Just show me where You want me to be."

Two weeks later, Sharon Knepp, the girlfriend of Gary's brother Dale, had returned from the mission in Guatemala. "Gary, I'm going to Macon, Mississippi, to visit Sharon," Dale told him. "I haven't seen her since I left Guatemala a month ago. Why don't you ride along and keep me company? You aren't up to helping Dad hang garage doors yet, anyway."

The brothers arrived in Macon just as a truck was leaving for the Troyers in Seymour, Missouri. It was loaded with a freezer the church at Macon had purchased for Marie.

"We've got an empty seat," the driver, Marie's uncle, called to Gary. "Want to ride along?"

Recalling Marie's letter saying that the children were having nightmares and were crying for him, Gary grabbed his suitcase, climbed into the truck, and headed for Missouri. The day he spent with Marie and her family was too short for the children. In the months Gary had boarded at their home in Palamá, he had become like an uncle to them. His presence had a healing and stabilizing effect on their wounded hearts.

Before Gary returned to Mississippi where his brother waited to return to North Carolina, the school board from the Grandin Christian School came to interview him. They had been trying to locate Gary to ask him to teach at their school, 120 miles from Seymour. Sensing God's leading, he accepted the position. School teaching would not be strenuous for his wounded shoulder.

Living 120 miles from the Troyer family allowed Gary to visit them on an occasional weekend. After spending happy evenings with the children, Gary and Marie would sit and talk and play games. Their conversation often turned to that traumatic night in Guatemala.

After the school year ended, Gary spent some time with his family in North Carolina. From there, he decided to go to Lamp and Light Publishing, a printing ministry, where he worked for six months in voluntary service.

* * * * *

Page after page was torn from the calendar of time. A sense of normality settled over the Troyer home. The caring kindnesses of acquaintances helped to ease the sharp pain of John's absence. Friends and relatives donated funds and labor to build a house for Marie in Seymour, across the road from her parents' home.

Each day Marie clung to the verse, "And we know that all things work together for good to them that love God, to them who are the called according to his purpose" (Romans 8:28).

Marie opened her eyes. What had wakened her? The glow of the clock displayed 11:50. The light of the full moon shone through the window. An icy shiver climbed her spine. For an instant she could almost hear the machetes slashing against the door and the angry shouts, punctuated with gunshots.

"Da-a-a-ady!" A heart-rending cry sliced through the night. "Da-addy-y-y-y!"

Marie pushed back the quilts. Nights were seldom peaceful. Nightmares haunted the children. Memories of the chilling scene had been painfully branded onto their young hearts.

Kneeling beside the cot, Marie stroked the sweated head. "What's wrong, honey? Are you having another dream?"

"They, they sh-shot my daddy and Gary and m-m-m-made them bleed," the young lad sobbed.

Marie held the child close. "It's just a dream, dear. No one is here. Just Mommy."

"I want my daddy!"

"He's with Jesus, darling." She squeezed the little hand.

"They killed Gary too," the little voice sobbed.

"No, dear, he got better. Remember?"

"I know he is dead like Daddy 'cause we never see him."

Marie sighed. "He came to see you several

times. Did you forget? Maybe he'll come see us again sometime."

"I wanna see him now!"

Struggling to keep her eyes open, Marie massaged the little back to relax the tense muscles. "We don't see Gary as often as we did when he taught school at Grandin. He lives in New Mexico now, where he helps to print papers to tell people about God. Maybe he'll come to see us again soon."

"Dear Father of the fatherless," Marie prayed softly, "help Your little one to rest well and to know Your angel is standing by his bed."

"Try to sleep now, dear. It will soon be time to get up for school," Marie whispered, patting the little head and flicking on the night light.

Unable to sleep, Marie curled up on the couch, wrapping an afghan about her. For several moments, she sat wrapped in silent thought. Soft carpet pillowed her feet beneath her slippers in contrast to the cold concrete she had been used to at Palamá. She thought of all the labor friends and relatives had donated to help with the erection of this house. She thought of the gifts of money, furniture, quilts, comforters, and other bedding. Then there was the donated freezer stocked with packages of meat and locker boxes of frozen vegetables and fruits. Stacks of cards had arrived in the mail. There had been visits as well as long distance phone calls to cheer the long evenings.

"O God!" she breathed. "You've provided for us far above what I could have imagined." Little did she know that God had more in store for her yet.

Switching on the lamp, Marie reached for her Bible. It fell open to John's memorial card.

She reread the words she had chosen to have printed on the inside:

> Why should I feel discouraged? Why should the shadows come?
> Why should my heart be lonely, and long for heaven and home?
> For Jesus is my comfort; my constant friend is He;
> His eye is on the sparrow, and I know He watches me.

Tucking the card between the pages of her Bible, Marie switched off the lamp and padded softly toward her bedroom.

The pale light of the full moon filtered through the curtains at the dining room window, bathing the chair at the head of the table in its silvery light. How empty the chair looked. The cavern in Marie's heart was filled with an empty ache for the one who would never sit at the head of her table again.

Weeks later, Marie received a letter with a

postmark from Farmington, New Mexico. She slit open the envelope, and a letter dropped into her hands. The signature was Gary's.

"I'll be traveling through Missouri," he had written in his neat handwriting. "I'd like to drop by and see your family again."

"Hurray!" the children shrieked when she told them. Each pitched in to do his part, sweeping floors, rolling out pie dough, and picking up toys.

When Gary walked through the door, he was attacked from every side by joyful shouts as little arms reached out to hug him.

Sitting at the head of the table, Gary asked God to bless the food. He spooned mashed potatoes onto little plates and served meat for the boys seated on either side of him chatting gaily. Sitting at the far end of the table, Marie buttered homemade bread for the twins who waved their spoons in their highchairs on either side of her. Marilyn passed the bowls of food from Timothy to her mother and ran to refill the water pitcher.

A happy feeling of completeness filled the air. Sensing this feeling, Timothy gazed at Gary with his large brown eyes. "Will you please be our daddy?" he asked earnestly.

You dear boy, Gary thought, longing to pull the little lad onto his lap.

Marie nearly dropped the salad bowl. Her

cheeks turned crimson as she busied herself with cutting the apple pie. *I hope Gary knows me well enough to know I didn't put that thought into Timothy's little head.*

When the last crumb of apple pie had been scraped from the plates, John Ray excused himself to start washing the dishes. Humming a little tune, Timothy cleared the table while Marie put the leftover food into containers. Marilyn washed Sharon and Karen's sticky hands and faces and sat down on the floor between them to show them a book.

Marie has trained them well, Gary thought as he picked up a dish towel to dry the dishes. *She knows how to keep a family happy.*

When the last dish was dried and put in its place, John Ray and Marilyn pulled the games from the closet.

After happy games of memory and dominoes, Gary pushed back his chair. "If you get me a book, I'll read to you." Having grown up in a family of ten, Gary loved children and had a special touch with them.

When Marie came into the living room, Gary was seated on an armchair, reading a Bible story with a twin on each knee, the boys on one arm of the chair, and Marilyn on the other.

The children would hardly leave Gary to go put on their pajamas. Only when he promised that he would come again, did the little ones go off to bed after kissing Gary good night. Somehow Marie knew there would be no nightmares tonight.

When the little teeth were brushed and the prayers said, Marie settled into the rocking chair across from Gary.

"So," Gary began gently, "tell me how you have been coping."

Marie looked at her hands lying in her lap. Her eyes filled with unbidden tears. "John's family and mine and friends from all over have been unbelievably generous and supportive. Yet I have to forgive John's murderers every day and keep trusting that God had a reason."

"And we know," Gary quoted, "that all things work together for good," Marie joined in, "to them that love God, to them who are the called according to his purpose."

"Don't ever forget that, Marie. Perhaps only eternity will reveal the full picture of who shot John, why they did it, and why God permitted it. Until then we must cling to that verse and rest in the confidence that it was not a mistake, but a part of God's plan."

He leaned back in his chair. "It's like the colors of a painting. The black clouds are oppressive by themselves, but when the brilliant hues of a sunrise are added to the picture, the painting is striking. The black clouds of our lives are not pleasant, but when we can see the whole picture in eternity, we will understand just why God put them there. We will see that it is the dark clouds that accent the rose and lavender of the sunrise. God did not promise that every circumstance in our lives would be pleasant, but that all the circumstances would work together for an ultimate good."

For several moments all was silent as each sat wrapped in thought.

Gary cleared his throat. "The mission board has asked me to go back to Guatemala to teach school for six months."

Marie grew pale. Closing her eyes, she saw John pleading, crying, and praying. She heard the thunderous crack and saw him fall. She stared mutely into the night seeing John's blood form a pool beneath him. She saw Gary lying so still as his life ebbed away. She saw the evil sneer on the murderer's lips and the cold, merciless eyes of steel.

Then in a flash, she saw the tears of 400 Indians. She felt the arms of the women about her as they sobbed on her shoulder. "We are so sad, Maria. John was our brother," she heard them cry.

Looking up, Marie asked, "You are planning to go?"

"I've told them I'll go. The Guatemalans need the Gospel as much as they ever did, and I know the language and the culture. Marie, as I lay on that mountain in Guatemala, looking up at the moon, I felt the blood ooze from me and felt my life slipping away. I told God, 'If You spare me, I'll serve You with everything I have.' He spared me, and I will keep my promise."

Gary gazed at Marie intently. "I'd like you to visit Guatemala while I am there."

Marie dropped her eyes. "I'll consider it, Gary. I'd like to take the children back again."

Rising to leave, Gary's eyes rested on the sweet face of the slender woman across from him. He knew he would return, and not only to see the children.

10

The Breaking of Dawn

Months later, tickets to Guatemala City were purchased for Marie and the five children.

"You are going back?" friends had asked in amazement.

"You have come back!" Marie could almost hear the Indians say in delight.

The wheels of the plane bounced lightly as they touched down on the runway. Marie was on Guatemalan soil once more.

"I want the children to see Palamá once again," Marie had told Robert and Lydia Byler who traveled with her. "I want them to see that what happened 18 months ago is past."

Yet the Bylers could tell by the excitement shining in her eyes that Marie was even more anxious to see Gary who was waiting in the airport. A part of her that had died had become alive again.

That evening, Gary helped get the little ones

dressed for bed and read them stories. It was evident from his ways with the children, that he had not grown up with six younger brothers and sisters in vain.

When Timothy began to say his prayers, Marie held her breath. *Please, don't let him say it tonight.*

"Dear God," he began. "Make the men who shot our daddy to stop being bad, and to get saved . . . and . . . and please give us a new daddy sometime. Amen."

"Oh, Son," Marie didn't dare to look into Gary's smiling eyes.

Everyone else at the mission house seemed to have found a reason to leave the living room. Marie and Gary were left alone with the flames that danced and crackled above the logs in the hearth.

How good it was to be with Gary again. How anxiously each had awaited the phone calls and letters, but there was nothing like being together.

As Gary gazed into Marie's eyes, she sensed what he was about to say. Her cheeks reddened as she lowered her eyes.

When Gary cleared his throat, Marie lifted her eyes to meet his gaze. "We've known each other a long time, Marie. Don't you think it's time we make some plans?"

The sweet smile lighting up her pleasant face

was his answer.

"My term is up in June. How soon can you get ready?" he asked.

The hours flew as details were discussed. "We may as well make our plans now," Gary told her. "International phone calls are expensive. I'll be coming home next month for my sister Jan's wedding. We can finalize some of the details then.

"Would you like William Bear to have the sermon?" he asked as he located a notebook and pen.

"That would be nice," Marie replied. "Then your dad could perform the ceremony. I'd like to have your sister Jan and Phil to be witnesses. Jan and I became close when she spent six weeks with me a year ago to help with the twins, you know."

"She put in a good word for you," Gary added with a smile. "Why don't we ask John's brother Nelson and his wife to be witnesses, too." He jotted a few lines in the notebook. "Could you make your good bread rolls for the ham and cheese sandwiches?"

"I guess I could. I could sew light blue dresses for the girls to match the dresses of those in the bridal party."

"I think it would be nice to have a special table for the children, your parents, John's, and mine. My little brothers could sit there too."

"That's a great idea, Gary. Do you think a quartet you sang with at Bible school could sing?"

"Probably could." Gary made a few notes, then closed his notebook. "Well, Marie, you've had a long day. We have a whole week left to talk," he told her with a smile. "I think it's time to say good night."

Only one week, Marie thought as she climbed the stairs. *I wish we wouldn't have to go back until Gary does.* But there were preparations that needed to be made. Time would go fast.

Sunday morning after everyone had left for services, Gary and Marie slipped over to the neighbors, who had a fountain in their courtyard, and posed for pictures before going on to church. No one must know their secret yet.

At the chapel, the Guatemalans welcomed Marie with open arms. How good it was to sing the Spanish songs again!

Sunday night, Lydia Byler told Marie, "I can tell Gary would like to spend some time alone with you. Let Robert and me put the children to bed for you tonight."

Marie's eyes lit up above her rosy cheeks. "Oh, thank you! Please call me if there is any problem."

"We'll get along fine. You just run along," Lydia replied.

After throwing another log onto the fire, Gary

turned to Marie. "How would you feel about going to Palamá with me next Sunday? Someone goes back for services there every six weeks. I thought we could go on Sunday if you are up to it."

Marie gave a little sigh. "I think it would be good for the children to see Palamá again and to realize that the trouble has passed." She gazed thoughtfully into the crackling flames. "Yes, we'll go. I'd love to see my brothers and sisters there again, and I've brought gifts to take along."

Suddenly the peace of the night was punctuated with the popping of fireworks.

"It sounds like someone is throwing a celebration for us," Gary grinned.

"More likely for the Pope who is visiting town," Marie smiled.

From upstairs came a shrill wail, followed by little sobs.

"The children!" Marie's eyes grew large. "They think the noises are gunshots!"

"Someone is shooting at us!" Timothy cried.

"No, honey," Lydia attempted to comfort the children who had been awakened from their sleep by the explosions. "It's just fireworks. No one is going to get hurt. Someone is just having a party."

"We don't like the noise either," Robert added, "but it won't hurt us."

When the sobs didn't subside, Marie told

Gary, "I'd better go talk to them. They think the guerillas are coming."

"Let me come along," Gary said rising from his chair. "After all, I'll soon be their daddy," he whispered, bounding up the stairs after her.

The sobs quieted the moment Gary opened the door. He talked to the children in his calm, kind voice, holding them, reassuring them, and encouraging the little ones to go back to sleep.

Timothy, as well as the other children, adored Gary. If Gary said the noise was nothing to be afraid of, then there was no reason to cry. With a few sniffs and sighs, the little ones nestled down once more. Perhaps if Timothy had known that his prayer would soon be answered, he would have been too excited to sleep.

Monday evening, Gary, Marie, and the children gathered around the table with Merle Yoder's family. "Happy birthday, dear Marilyn," they sang as the six-year-old blew out the candles on the Raggedy Ann cake her mother had decorated for her. Marie wanted to be sure the children would take happy memories of Guatemala back to the United States this time.

When Marie went to the market with Merle's wife Susan, days later, the sights, sounds, and smells brought back a surge of memories of the country that had become dear to her heart.

There was the sound of bartering:

"Tres quetzales."

"Dos."

"Tres!"

"Dos y cinquenta."

Brilliantly dressed Indians sat on the ground beside the produce and goods they had spread on the ground around them. The air was filled with the scent of overripe fruit and freshly cut flowers. Flies clustered on the bare hunks of meat that hung from the stalls. Beaming children gathered around Marie, trying to sell her their trinkets. The verdant mountains towered in the background beneath the cloudless sky.

"Oh, Susan!" Marie exclaimed. "This country is still in my blood."

* * * * *

As the mountainside awoke with the first pastel rays of dawn and the mist floated behind the ridges, a Blazer slowly wound its way over the rugged road. Iridescent birds sang to their mates from their leafy perches. Brilliant flowers lifted their fragile heads to greet the rising sun.

As the Blazer crawled up a steep ridge, John Ray called out as his father always had, "Give it the berries!"

When Marie and the children climbed out of the Blazer, the Indians stared in disbelief. "You've come!" they cried in a joyous welcome. "You've come back!"

"I've come," Marie replied, as she returned

the embrace of her sisters. "I've come because I love you."

As Marie led the children to the little church, Gary walked at her side. For a moment Marie turned to gaze at the hallowed spot where John and Gary's blood had soaked the earth. Seeing the house that had once sheltered their happy family, Marie struggled to control the tears that welled up and threatened to overflow any minute.

Gary looked at Marie's pale face with concern. "Are you going to be all right?" he questioned gently.

"I think so," Marie smiled feebly. "There were so many memories that came rushing back. I just needed to deal with the feelings and forgive again."

Hearing her name, Marie turned to see who had called. "Emiliana!" she cried falling into her friend's arms. "You've remained faithful!"

"Of course," Emiliana smiled with a glow spreading across her tan cheeks. "Have you heard Alejandro and I are getting married this week?"

"Alejandro! The school teacher! Oh, Emiliana, I'm so happy. I wish I could stay for the wedding, but we can't change our flights."

Sitting on a bench in the chapel and seeing the pulpit John had preached from was not as difficult as Marie had feared. The vibrant singing of the beaming Guatemalans helped to heal that ache. *"Bienvenido! Bienvenido!"* the villagers sang with gusto. "Welcome! Welcome!"

With great joy and pleasure,
We've returned today.
We clasp your hands once more;
Our hearts overflow with love.
Together we give thanks to God.

Thus far God has helped you,
Never a moment left you,
And to us you have returned;
Welcome!

. . . In the eternal gathering,
There will be no separation,
No sadness nor affliction.

Welcome! Welcome!
The brethren here today,
Joyfully we say, Welcome! Welcome!
As we meet again. Welcome!

John and I could have lived safely in Michigan, Marie thought. *But would Emiliana and Alejandro and all the others be sitting in this chapel, singing so joyfully if we had stayed at home?*

As the Blazer wound down the mountain,

Marie's heart was filled with peace as she thought, *John would have wanted us to take this trip to show the Guatemalans that we care about them in spite of what their countrymen did a year and a half ago. He would have wanted his children to return to Palamá to deal with painful memories and to feel the healing love and forgiveness toward those whose people had killed their father.* It was as though the visit to Palamá put the final sentence on a chapter in Marie and the children's lives. The past had been laid to rest, and a new chapter had begun.

God had not healed the bleeding hearts in one instantaneous touch. But He was closing the wounds one stitch at a time with His healing needle of love. The first sutures placed on the gaping wounds were stitched with the kindnesses of friends. God's presence, and verses from His Word, had been a healing balm. It was as if the love exchanged between the Indians and the Troyer family on this trip to Guatemala, and to Palamá in particular, was the thread that was needed to suture the last of the wounds. Perhaps the final knot that held all the sutures in place, was Gary's caring supportiveness. A thin scar would always remain, but the bleeding from the wounded hearts had diminished.

That night, the light shone from Gary's window. It was nearly midnight, but he could not sleep. As he sat on his bed with his pen in his hand, staring into the darkness beyond the window, he thought of that fateful Sunday night, 18 months before. He relived the feelings of fear, pain, and grief that the visit to Palamá had awakened. He thought of how he had wished he could have died and John could have lived. He thought of Marie, how brave she had been, the way she had reached out to help others in spite of her own grief.

He thought about how God had directed the events in his life, leading him to Guatemala and so clearly directing the events after his return to North Carolina. There was his unplanned trip to Missouri and God's leading him to teach at Grandin.

His thoughts turned to the future, causing the feelings in his heart to overflow into the words of a poem which he jotted onto his tablet.

As the plane revved its engines in preparation for takeoff early Monday morning, Marie pressed her face against the window, straining to see Gary waving in the darkness. "Please keep him safe, dear God," she prayed.

A warm contentment filled the dark cavern in her heart as she recalled the cozy evening she had shared with Gary beside the fireplace at the mission house.

As the plane rose above the majestic mountains and volcanoes, into the velvety blackness studded with sparkling stars, Marie switched on

the small overhead light. Opening the poem
Gary had pressed into her hand before she left,
she read with bated breath.

> Unerringly God has directed our paths,
>   and faithfully guided our ways.
> For His tender leading and unfailing
>   care,
>   our hearts are filled with praise.
>
> A companion and guide o'er life's rugged
>   way,
>   He has helped us each mountain to
>   climb;
> Then to face the future, though to us
>   unknown,
>   and leave those mountains behind.
>
> Now together He's brought us from sepa-
>   rate ways,
>   to make us a threefold cord;
> United firmly and bonded by love,
>   together and with the Lord.

Tears filled Marie's eyes as she folded the
poem. "O God," she breathed. "You've been so
good."

Resting her cheek against the soft hair of the
sleeping toddler in her arms, Marie whispered,
"Only four more months and you'll have a daddy

again! Only four more months!"

From behind the ridges, dawn pushed up the shroud of darkness, tinting the sky with a rosy glow, chasing night's shadows away.

As her tears blurred the colors of the sunrise, Marie knew that God was painting a lovely sunrise on the lonely night of her soul. And as Gary had said, the clouds that hung in the background would only heighten the hues of the painting.

Ten Years Later— September 1991

The sands of months and years trickled through the hourglass of time until it was September once again, September 1991.

The setting sun cast its last golden rays on a cozy home nestled in a grove of pines in an area called the Grassy Ridge of North Carolina. On the mailbox surrounded with flowers were the handpainted names of Gary and Marie Miller.

From a recording of the Grassy Ridge Quartet, a singing ministry Gary was a part of, these words drifted through the open windows:

Blessed be the name of Jesus, our Redeemer dear above,
Who is making home so happy with the blessing of His love . . .
He will lead us all to Glory, if we lean upon His grace.

Let us live with Him forever in the
sunlight of His face.

The music drifting from the house was evidence that God had given "beauty for ashes, the
oil of joy for mourning, the garment of praise for
the spirit of heaviness." He had wrought hope
from heartbreak and happiness out of tragedy.

From the back yard floated shouts of happy
laughter as Timothy and John Ray sailed above
the trampoline, while their younger brother,
three-year-old Christopher Gary bounced and
tumbled beside them. The ten-year-old twins,
Sharon and Karen were reading a book together
in the tree-shaded lawn beside the trampoline.
Humming along with the music that came from
the house, Marilyn helped her sister, six-year-
old Jessica Marie with a needlework project.

On the back porch swing, Gary and Marie
shared the events of the day as the chain of the
swing squeaked its protest to the gentle rhythmic movement. While Marie listened to Gary
tell about the activities at the office of the family
overhead door business which both he and John
Ray were involved in, her heart treasured the
sounds of laughter coming from the yard beyond
the porch.

There was a peaceful air about the home, a
peace that had had its shapings, no doubt, in the
fires of tragedy. Perhaps it was the former

heartbreak that made the home aware that each family member is a priceless gift from God, and not a moment of family life is meant to be marred with friction.

Nor was an evening of family life to be wasted when memories could be made, and relationships built.

Gary called to the boys, telling them that if they would gather some twigs and branches, the family would roast hot dogs. While the boys hurried to stack the wood, the girls ran inside to collect the hot dogs, marshmallows, and other supplies.

The orange flames shone against the twilight with a warm golden glow as the family gathered around the fire. Sizzling hot dogs dangled from the ends of sharpened sticks.

As Timothy gazed into the leaping flames, his face reflecting the orange glow, he thought of the night at Palamá. Though thoughts of that night no longer haunted him, a few unanswered questions of what had taken place ten years before still troubled him.

Turning to Gary, he asked, "Dad, whatever happened to the men who shot you and my father John?"

With his stick, Gary poked at the fire before answering. "Well, Son," he began. "Villagers have said that the guerilla commander who shot us was killed in a skirmish in recent years. Yet it's hard to know for sure."

For a long moment there was only the sound of crackling flames.

"You know," Timothy's freckled face was thoughtful. "I used to want to grow up fast so I could find those men and kill them, but Mother kept reminding me to pray for them, and somehow praying for them made that hate go away. It makes me feel kind of sad now to think one of them might have died without knowing God." Stroking the dog at his side, he continued, "But I still wonder why—why did they do it?"

Gary gazed into the western horizon. "O God!" he breathed. "The boy deserves an answer."

Facing Timothy, he began. "That's a question I battled with for a long time. If you would have been a little older you would have known that Palamá is in that lawless part of the country where greed or simply a whispered grudge could motivate a raid. Knowing exactly what triggered this attack is something we can only guess at. It seems the only definite answer we have at this point is that God allowed it, and allowed it for a purpose."

Looking reflectively into the dusk, Gary continued, "When I saw the gun aimed at your father, I thought I had to stop those bullets. But all I could do was to stand there clenching and unclenching my fists in desperation while I prayed for God's will to be done."

"You couldn't have stopped them or you would both have been killed!" Timothy inserted. "You did the next best thing, you took care of Daddy's family for him. Grandpa and Grandma Troyer have said that if it was God's time for their son to die, they are glad you were willing to take care of his family. Grandma said it's like they have gained a son."

"Children," Gary placed an arm around Timothy's shoulder as he addressed the three teenagers and the twins. "Children, there was a quote in your father's Bible that I want you never to forget. 'If we want to die for Christ, we must first live for Him.'"

He paused, looking up into the darkening sky. "That became very real to me as I lay on the cold ground, wounded, not knowing whether I would live or die. I promised to serve God with all my energy for the rest of my life."

"Maybe that's why you and Mother spend so much time with Pasquels and the other Mexican neighbors," Sharon suggested as she coaxed a sticky toasted marshmallow from the end of a stick.

Gary drained his glass of cider before replying. "Mother and I prayed about a life to touch, and God led us to Celia and Pasquel. They had just immigrated from Mexico, remember? And Celia couldn't speak any English. When we helped them butcher, and when Mother sewed for Celia and translated her Spanish at the doctor's office, we tried to show them God's love. We prayed for their salvation. One soul is worth more than all the wealth in the world. That's why we helped Uncle Dale's family and others start the Spanish church services for Pasquels and the other Mexicans in the community."

"You know," Marie's voice was soft. "One of the happiest moments in my life was when I saw Celia respond to William Bear's invitation to accept Christ—and then to hear Daddy translate her testimony: 'I'm so glad God saved me! I'm so glad He forgave my sins!'

"Nothing can be more rewarding than helping others find Jesus. That night at Palamá when I thought we might all lose our lives, our few material possessions lost all their value. I learned in a deeper way that souls are what count in life, not the accumulation of goods."

The western sky glowed with vivid streaks of gold, pink, and lavender as if an immense brush had painted them using the sky as its easel. The clouds that swirled and billowed high in the western sky gave depth and character to the colors on the horizon. The dark pines stood silhouetted against the sunset while fireflies winked beneath their boughs like a hundred tiny stars.

Jessica looked up at her father with an intense

expression on her young face. "What happened to the Christians when the missionaries went away?"

Gary slapped at a mosquito that had landed on his arm. "At first missionaries went back every six weeks to help encourage the churches at Palamá and Paquib. Then when it became safer, missionaries moved back to Palamá."

"Weren't Merle and Bill ambushed on the way back from Paquib?" John Ray questioned as he reached for the bag of marshmallows.

"Tell us about it, Daddy!" the children begged, leaning forward. "Tell us about it!"

"Well," Gary cleared his throat. "It was several months after the attack at Palamá. Bill Byler and Merle Yoder had been to Paquib to encourage the Christians there. Warned that it was unsafe for them to stay overnight, the missionaries headed out the lonely trail on their cycles. They rode down into a hollow, and Bill was just lowering the front tire of his cycle into a stream when two men jumped out from behind the bushes.

"'*Alto! Alto!*' they yelled. ('Stop! Stop!') One of the men swung a machete while the other waved a gun. 'You are rich Americans taking advantage of us poor Indians!' they shouted. They robbed Bill and Merle, then released them shouting, 'Go home Yankees and never come back!'

"Bill pulled several tracts from his pocket and

offered them to the men. 'If you'll read these,' he told them, 'you'll see we aren't here for the reasons you think.'

"Bill told me later that after he and Merle were released, they took off out of that hollow as fast as their cycles would take them. At the top of the ridge, they knelt to thank God for His protection."

"Those missionaries were brave!" Karen exclaimed, her eyes wide.

"So were the other missionaries who moved back to Palamá several years later," Marie began, as she held Christopher closer in the coolness of nightfall. "My cousin Titus told me there were nights they didn't know if they'd live to see the sun rise again."

"They moved to Chimaltenango and then back to the States, didn't they?" Timothy asked.

"That's right," Marie replied. "Their lives were being threatened, and the church pled with them to leave for the sake of safety."

"But what happened to the Christians at Palamá?" Sharon wanted to know.

Gary gazed into the twilight. "It's been about a year now since they chose to relocate rather than to compromise their convictions. Villagers formed a night watch against the guerillas and tried to force the Christians to help patrol.

"'We can't take part in the night watch,' the Christians said, 'That would violate Christ's teachings on loving our enemies and on nonresistance. But we can continue to serve the community in other ways.'

"The Christians were threatened with imprisonment and even with death if they did not cooperate, but that didn't faze them. 'You can put us in jail,' they replied, 'but we can't take part in night watch.'

"Oh!" Jessica exclaimed. "And did they have to go to jail?"

"Well, one of the Christians was put in jail for a while," her father replied. "Then finally, under the constant pressure to compromise, and because they feared for their lives, eight Christian families decided to relocate. Emiliana and Alejandro and their children were with those who chose to leave homes, crops, jobs, and inherited lands rather than to violate their convictions. The church is now settled in Tecpan."

"I'm so glad Emiliana and the others stayed faithful." Marilyn's voice was soft as she looked at the round orange moon that had risen above the pines. A chorus of insects chirped in the meadow. The frogs in the ditch, with their throaty croaking, joined the night serenade while a cool breeze whispered through the leaves overhead.

Marie's voice was thoughtful. "The Christians from Palamá made the statement, 'We have left our earthly homes to gain a heavenly one.'"

Gary nodded adding, "We may never know

what effect John's life and his dying testimony, 'For to me to live is Christ and to die is gain' may have had on the church from Palamá."

He paused for a moment and then continued with a quote from Jim Elliot, "'He is no fool who gives what he cannot keep to gain what he cannot lose.'"

The glowing embers of the fire burned lower. As the stars flickered on one by one, the last shades of sunset faded into the blue of night. Softly, Marie began to sing, and her family joined in.

Will there be any stars, any stars in my
  crown,
When at evening the sun goeth down?
When I wake with the blest in the man-
  sions of rest,
Will there be any stars in my crown?

The sun had set behind the pines but dawn glowed within the hearts of the family. Together they awaited the most glorious dawning of all, beyond the sunset of life, when they would meet their Saviour and the loved ones who waited in the land of eternal dawn.

Christian Light Publications, Inc., is a non-profit conservative Mennonite publishing company providing Christ-centered, Biblical literature in a variety of forms including Gospel tracts, books, Sunday school materials, summer Bible school materials, and a full curriculum for Christian day schools and home schools.

For more information at no obligation or for spiritual help, please write to us at:

Christian Light Publications, Inc.
P.O. Box 1126
Harrisonburg, VA 22801-1126